GOD SPEED THE PLOUGH

Wesley Wyatt has been farming near Wiveliscombe for over 70 years. His career both spans and reflects the dramatic changes in agricultural policy and rural life over that period. Taking over the family farm at the age of 18, he transformed it from an old-fashioned mix of corn and beef into one of the most intensive and successful farm businesses in Somerset, surviving all manner of trials and tribulations along the way, before easing back and turning to conservation in his later years.

A strict Methodist upbringing, a well-developed social conscience and an upright but outgoing personality have led him into many other avenues, from golf through local politics to his beloved Old Tauntonians, encountering many unlikely characters along the way. All of this makes for a life story which is as rich as it is compelling, beautifully illustrated by over 40 photographs. Wesley Wyatt's endeavours may indeed have been unpredictable, but that makes them all the more fascinating.

Anthony Gibson was for many years the South-West Regional Director of the National Farmers' Union. He was awarded an OBE for services to the rural community in 2003.

GOD SPEED THE PLOUGH

A Story of Unpredictable Endeavour

Wesley Wyatt

with best wishes to Sue & Adam
Wesley

CHARLCOMBE BOOKS

Charlcombe Books
125 Garnet Street, Bristol BS3 3JH
tel: 01174 523760

First published 2023

ISBN: 978 1 7399293 2 9

Printed and bound in Great Britain by
CPI Antony Rowe, Bumpers Farm, Chippenham SN14 6LH

Contents

To Olive,
with love and thanks

Acknowledgements

My grateful thanks go to: my daughter Jayne, son Robert, Sue Farrington, Sue Mitchell, Eileen Smith, Edward Traugott, Barry Cottrell, and Taunton School Foundation for photographs; and to Anthony Gibson and Stephen Chalke for their encouragement and advice.

Introduction

by Anthony Gibson

This is the story of a West Somerset farmer spanning nine decades. But not just any West Somerset farmer. Wesley Wyatt has always led the way, whether it was in maximum productivity in the 1950s and 60s, in achieving scale through co-operation in the 70s and 80s, through to making space for nature in the 2000s and beyond. Go-ahead farmer he may have been, but there has been an old-fashioned, in the best sense, public spiritedness and concern for his fellow man about the many other aspects of his life. Brought up a Methodist, he played the organ in his local chapel for over 30 years. He has served on every conceivable organisation in his local community. He transformed the fortunes of Burnham and Berrow Golf Club. He has been a pillar of the Old Tauntonians for over 40 years. And he even, on one famous occasion, burnt down a church on the instructions of the churchwarden.

Then there are the characters he has encountered in his long life. Not least George, the Kenyan who turned up in Taunton hoping for a career in nursing, was taken in by the Wyatt family and became both a lifelong friend and a living legend in the British army; and Uncle Henry, the German hairdresser who married Wesley's great aunt Nell on the day before the First World War broke out and was interned on the Isle of Man. Their stories are told vividly as well.

I first met Wesley in March 1978, a few days after his nearly-new sheep shed had collapsed under the weight of eight feet of snow, killing more than 50 heavily pregnant ewes, some of them so badly hurt that they had been destroyed by Wesley himself, with a humane killer borrowed from the vet. Gallantly he was giving interviews to the local press. A television reporter asked him if his losses would be covered by insurance. "Insurance?" he exploded. "Why should I be interested in insurance, when the welfare of my livestock is my only concern?" And he meant it. That was the mark of the man he is.

Wesley Wyatt has farmed through two revolutions in British farming in his 74-year farming career. When his grandfather unexpectedly left him the farm just outside Wiveliscombe in West Somerset in 1946 and he was brought home from school to run it in 1948, production at all costs was not merely the farmer's aim, it was his duty. The ink on the 1947 Agriculture Act, committing government and farmers alike to greater self-sufficiency, the lessons of the War having been learned, was hardly dry. This chimed very happily with Wesley's own instincts. His father was an easy-going sort, quite content that only about two-thirds of his 100 or so acres was farmable, the rest being taken up by boggy ground, elderly cider orchards and a network of hedges so dense that average field size was barely four acres. Farmer Dick, Wesley's father, loved his hedges. Farmer Wes had no time for them, especially when the first task he was given when he was summoned home from school was to cut them all back, ready for harvest, by hand, with a staff hook, at the height of a hot summer.

So as soon as he was in charge he set to work draining the wetland, straightening and canalising the Hillfarrance Brook, grubbing up the orchards and bulldozing the hedges, generously assisted in every case by Ministry of Agriculture grants. Within just a few years, the slopes of Croford Hill, between the Taunton to Barnstaple railway and the old A361, were transformed from a pastoral arcadia to an arable prairie.

All of this destruction, as it would probably be regarded nowadays, is related by Wesley without a hint of shame or remorse. Unlike his father, he was an ambitious farmer, keen to make the most of all of the government grants and advice that were available, in his own and, as it was seen at the time, the national interest. Having turned Hillacre Farm into an economic unit, his next aim was to expand and, like many another young farmer in the 50s and 60s, he wasn't afraid of building his business on borrowed money. First came a pig enterprise, then two nearby farms were snapped up and then, again very much in the spirit of the times, came co-operation, first in the shape of a potato growing and marketing group with neighbouring farmers and then full-scale farm amalgamation with Chris Shapland, just over the hill at Fitzhead.

This was in the 70s, after the UK had joined the EEC and become associated with its surpluses, and serious doubts were just beginning to be voiced as to whether the policy of all-out production, at the expense of serious damage to the countryside, really made much sense any more. Wesley was beginning to have doubts as well, especially when heavy rain washed hundreds of tons of topsoil off his sloping prairie and into the Hillfarrance Brook. Maybe it was time to put some of the hedges back, running along the contours to keep the soil in place.

If that was a pragmatist's approach to finding an accommodation between productivity and conservation, then Chris Shapland's was that of a true believer. It would probably be putting it too strongly to say that he made a convert of his partner, but Wesley was happy enough to go along with all of the tree-planting, hedge restoration and soil management which Chris initiated. So impressive were the results that Fitzhead Farms, as their partnership was known, won the Bronze Otter award, given by the Somerset Farming and Wildlife Advisory Group (FWAG) for combining efficient farming with intelligent conservation in 1988. Wesley now has his own Countryside Stewardship agreement, under which the wetland that he drained in the 1950s is being re-wetted, new hedges are being planted and land is being set aside for wildflower pasture. The wheel has not quite come full circle, because most of the farm is still being very efficiently farmed under a contract arrangement, but the two revolutions – the revolution in production of the 1950s and 60s and the counter-revolution in putting nature back into farming of the 1980s onwards – form the agricultural framework of Wesley Wyatt's story.

Wesley was not just in tune with the farming times, he was very often ahead of them; an innovator, a leader of opinion, widely recognised as one of the best farmers in the West of England, as witnessed by Fitzhead Farms being judged as the best large farming business in Somerset in 1985 and 1986, shortly before it was recognised for its conservation work. Unlike many of his fellow farmers, he understood the value of co-operation and partnership. He recruited to the business two of the best stockmen in the South-West in John Smith, his head shepherd, and John Thompson, his pig manager, and, recognising their value, he and Chris took them into the partnership. He was a great believer in research and made the very most of it, not only in his own farming but in spreading the gospel more widely. As Chairman of the Advisory Committee at the Liscombe Experimental Husbandry Farm on Exmoor, he helped livestock farmers throughout the region save money and boost productivity. And when the government provocatively decided to close it down in 1989, he led a successful farmer-funded rescue.

But though he was a farmer first and foremost, there has been much more to Wesley Wyatt than that. Take that Christian name, for example. He was actually christened Richard, like his father and great grandfather before him, but his parents were strict Methodists and what better name could there be for a young dissenter than Wesley? His mother, one of the two greatest influences in his life, who was much stricter in her devotions than his easy-going father, insisted on Wesley taking the Pledge, and he played the organ in Wiveliscombe's Methodist Chapel, man and boy, for over 30 years. God would surely speed his plough.

And if he hasn't quite managed to stick to his pledge and has thrown in his lot with the Church of England, he remains highly principled, setting and expecting in return the highest standards of courtesy, good manners and consideration and respect for others: all qualities learned from his family background but reinforced by the other great influence in his life, Donald Crichton-Miller, legendary headmaster when Wesley was at Taunton School, but a great friend in later life, not least through the Old Tauntonians.

The outcomes of Wesley's endeavours have sometimes been not just unpredictable but painful. He's had his downs as well as ups. Besides the collapse of his sheep-shed, there was the great fire in the early 1960s, when he lost his entire wheat crop on Croford Hill; a spark from a passing steam train set the whole lot on fire, leaving nothing but scorched earth. His first marriage ended in divorce, amid much local disapproval, although he has now found lasting happiness with his second wife Olive. The Fitzhead Farms partnership broke up when the younger generation of Wyatts and Shaplands decided that they wanted to go it alone, with Wesley not even allowed a say in the decision. And in the aftermath of that setback, a disease outbreak wiped out his pig unit and left him struggling to avoid bankruptcy.

Sport has been a big part of his life, whether that be Wiveliscombe RFC, Somerset County Cricket Club or Burnham and Berrow Golf Club, which he helped save from financial disaster, before going on to earn the singular honour of being its Captain in its centenary year of 1990. At 90 he still plays golf every Wednesday morning at Burnham, come rain or shine, frost or tempest, in the Stocks Foursomes group. He plays his golf rather as he has lived his life – decisively! Straight-backed, he marches up the fairways, a picture of no-nonsense determination, barely breaking his stride as he thumps another shot towards the green, invariably good-humoured but with a distinctly competitive streak when the chips are down, and always that Wesley Wyatt hallmark of a firm friendly handshake when the game is done.

For all his farming achievements, Wesley Wyatt is no gentleman farmer, with all the connotations of that label. He is a working farmer, who affects no airs and graces and is no lover of hunting or shooting. What he most certainly is, is a gentlemanly farmer, who brings as much courtesy and consideration to his relations with his fellow human beings as he has brought skill and dedication to his farming, It has been a great privilege for me to have been able to help him tell his story – a story which may indeed have been one of 'unpredictable endeavour' but which has also been one of such distinction and interest as to deserve the widest possible audience.

1

Of farming stock

I suppose I was born to be a farmer. For farming was certainly in my blood. Looking back over 200 years and more, I would struggle to name any of my forebears who was not a farmer or did not come from a farming family.

The most distant Wyatt of whom we have any knowledge was my great-great-grandfather, Robert Wyatt, born in 1801. He was, as far as we know, a Somerset man but he married a Devonshire wife, Prudence Bowerman. It must have been a good marriage, as Prudence came with two farms, just across the county boundary in the Blackdown Hills: Culmbridge Farm at Hemyock and Blackaller Farm, not far from the Wellington Monument. Whether Robert had an interest in what would become my farming home of Hillacre when he married Prudence, we don't know, but he was certainly farming Hillacre as a tenant in 1865. Prudence outlived both her husband and their son Richard so that, when she died in 1897, she left Culmbridge to her grandson, another Robert, and Blackaller to his elder brother, John Redwood Wyatt. Robert was clearly more at home in Somerset than in Devon as no sooner had he inherited the farm than he sold it, so that he could buy Hillacre as the sitting tenant. By this time he had married Sarah Dinham, who was one of eight brothers and sisters, brought up at Fry's Farm, which adjoins Hillacre, and who was doubtless another factor in Grandfather Wyatt's decision to cut his ties with the Blackdowns.

On my mother's side of the family, one of my earliest memories is of Granny Burge, my maternal great-grandmother. I only met her late in her life, when she was living at Providence, upstream from Sampford Brett. But Granny Burge is most strongly connected in my mind with Clicket, a hamlet in a deep wooded valley near Timberscombe, which once boasted a mill, two lime quarries with associated kilns, and an unofficial nonconformist chapel, as well as numerous scattered dwellings. It is now just a collection of picturesque ruins, having been abandoned around the turn of the twentieth century, and of documentary evidence that the family lived at Clicket there is no trace. Nonetheless, my relatives on my mother's side always make a point of visiting Clicket whenever they come to Somerset, and I built some timber from the Clicket water-wheel into a wall at Hillacre, so the connection lives on. Granny Burge and her husband George had a family of eight children, of whom the eldest daughter Emma married John Reed. He had started adult life as a farm worker at Clapton but, by dint of hard work and dedication, was able to move on to farming in his own right, first at Jenkins Farm, Rodhuish and eventually at Burcher's Farm, Milverton. He and Emma produced seven children: my mother Elsie, Wesley who was drowned in New Zealand, Winifred, Ethel, Florence and two sons, George and Bert.

My parents' wedding day
Back: Granny Wyatt, Grandfather Wyatt, Father, Mother,
Granny Reed, Leslie Greenway, Grandfather Reed
Front: unknown, Ethel, Florence, Winifred (Mother's sisters)

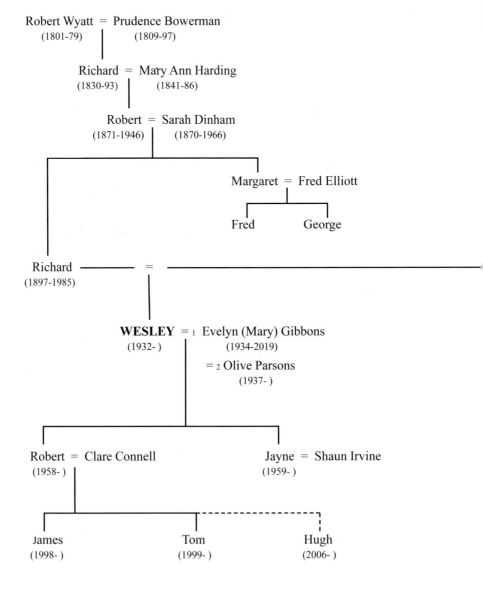

Robert Wyatt = Prudence Bowerman
(1801-79)   (1809-97)

Richard = Mary Ann Harding
(1830-93)   (1841-86)

Robert = Sarah Dinham
(1871-1946)   (1870-1966)

Margaret = Fred Elliott

Fred   George

Richard ———— =
(1897-1985)

WESLEY =1 Evelyn (Mary) Gibbons
(1932-)   (1934-2019)

=2 Olive Parsons
(1937-)

Robert = Clare Connell   Jayne = Shaun Irvine
(1958-)   (1959-)

James   Tom   Hugh
(1998-)   (1999-)   (2006-)

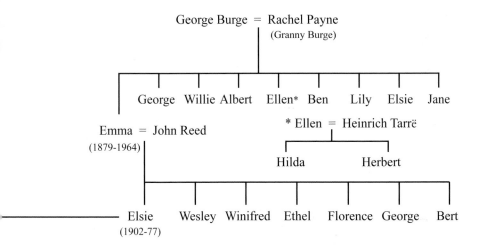

Family Tree

The second Burge daughter, who I always knew as Auntie Nell, was responsible for starting what I always think of as the Dutch wing of the family. In 1913 she met a man called Heinrich Tarrë, originally from Leipzig, who had set up in business as a hairdresser in Torquay, German hairdressers being quite the thing in Edwardian England, and was in West Somerset to visit friends. They fell in love; he moved his business to Minehead and changed his name to Henry. After overcoming resistance from her parents, they married in St Mary's, Stogumber on August 3rd 1914, the day before Britain declared war on Germany!

There was no immediate internment of German nationals, other than those who were regarded as a threat to national security, but the following summer, after the sinking of the Lusitania by a German U-boat, public anger was such that a policy of general internment was introduced. Uncle Henry, as he would become known, was sent to Knockaloe Camp on the Isle of Man, along with 23,000 other 'aliens', prisoner number 21839. He never talked about the experience on the several occasions when I met him, but he seems to have coped pretty well, becoming barber to the camp commander and his staff officers, which gave him privileges and a small income. He was even allowed to keep a pet dog, Prince, as can be seen from the photograph taken at the camp.

Aunt Nell was also technically an 'alien', by virtue of her marriage. British-born wives married to Germans were encouraged by the authorities to divorce their husbands, in which case they could keep their possessions and money. But Aunt Nell refused, meaning that she had to report monthly to her local police station, and what little money she had was confiscated. In 1918, after the Armistice, she was shipped off to Germany where she and Henry were eventually reunited. On his way back to Germany Henry had been well-treated in Holland, and that is where he decided he wanted to set up in business. This they did, together with Henry's brother Otto, as hairdressers and perfumiers, with a shop in one of the main city streets. They must have done very well, for when I visited the shop many years later it had 'By Royal Appointment to Queen Wilhelmina' proudly posted over the door.

Henry Tärre at Knockaloe Camp, with his dog Prince

Nell and Henry had two children, Hilda and Herbert, my second cousins, whom I came to know well. At one point Nell suggested to Herbert that he take me to Germany, to visit Leipzig and other places associated with his father's family. But Herbert was having none of it. "You know, mother, that I will never set foot in Germany," was his only reply. It turned out that, during the Second World War, he had worked for the resistance in the Netherlands, surviving on tulip bulbs and hiding under floorboards, and he hated Germans with a passion. On one visit he took me on his moped to a sandy area near Sheveningen where he had witnessed 50 or so civilians, taken from the local prison, being shot every day. No wonder he hated the Germans!

In 1960 Uncle Henry himself took me on a visit to Brussels. It was quite an eye-opener. First I was amazed at how the city had been re-built in the space of just 15 years after being left in ruins at the end of the war. And even more amazing were the public toilet arrangements, with a lady at a desk taking your money as you went in, ideally placed to survey all the goings on – which included Uncle Henry shouting out "bugger", on discovering that he'd got his long johns on back to front on going into a cubicle to have a pee!

Aunt and Uncle would come to Providence every so often to catch up with the rest of the family, Nell staying with her mother, and Uncle Henry taking himself off to the Egremont Hotel in Williton where he could have a drink and smoke his cigars in peace. For as long as my grandmother was alive, there were also regular family get-togethers at Providence, when Aunt Nell would arrive from Holland, Aunt Polly from Bristol, Aunt Elsie from Liverpool, Uncle Ben from

Standing: Uncle Bert, Granny, Aunt Nell, Auntie Polly, Uncle Ben
Seated: Auntie Elsie, Auntie Lily, Auntie Dot

Sampford Brett and Aunt Lily from Washford. Uncle Will, who was Aunt Lill's husband, was head gardener at Nettlecombe Court. Mother and I visited Uncle Ben at the end of his life when he was in Musgrove Park Hospital. The date was May 5th. I remember it because May 5th was 'bean day' and Uncle Ben asked me if I had planted my runner beans.

My cousin Fred Elliott farmed just a couple of miles away at Oakhampton. He and his brother George were the sons of my father's sister Margaret, whom I always knew as Auntie Mar. Fred would go on to do great things with the NFU, for which he was awarded the CBE. She clearly had her father's genes because she was kind, soft-hearted and very appreciative of the kindness of others. Sadly, because of the occasional bout of epilepsy, she was confined in Tone Vale Hospital for much of her life, something which today we would regard as unnecessary and shameful.

Son George took her out and we collected her for Sunday lunch fairly regularly for which she was always grateful. She accepted life in the institution without complaint, and when in later life she had a leg amputated she never grumbled.

Fred and I had a regular appointment, August 1st each year, his birthday, when I would drive over to Oakhampton and we would sit in our respective vehicles and have a long, farmer-to-farmer chat. He had served with distinction in Burma during the war but never really talked about his experiences until, out of the blue, on his 90th birthday, he suddenly came out with: "The atomic bomb saved my life." What he meant was that if the war with Japan had continued, he might well have been killed in Burma. As it was, he lived to a ripe old age, although he too had had his share of mental problems earlier in his life.

2

Early years

I was born at Edbrookes, the cottage on Hillacre Farm where my parents were living, with my father's mother and father in the main farm house, in the hamlet of Croford about a mile and a half east of Wiveliscombe, on 16 April 1932. I remember quite clearly what was, by modern standards, a distinctly primitive environment: oil lamps, water pumped from the well, outside toilet and bath water heated by a wood and coal-fired boiler which was carried to the kitchen on a Friday evening. There was an empty cottage to the rear of the main farmhouse, which was where I would ride my treasured tricycle.

Family life in those early years seemed to revolve mostly around chapel and gardening. Both of my parents, Richard (always known as Dick) and Elsie, were devout Methodists, my mother especially so. Every Sunday we would walk twice to Wiveliscombe Chapel, first

Father, Mother and me

Granny Reed, me, Mother and (seated) Great Granny Burge

for the 11 o'clock service and then again for the 6.30 gathering, with Sunday School, which my mother organised for the Croford youngsters, occupying most of the afternoon. Thursday evenings were reserved for midweek chapel. If my mother's faith was deep and serious, father's had its lighter moments. I remember one Sunday morning coming out of chapel holding his hand when the preacher asked him, "Are you saved, Brother?" Father replied, "I'm the only one saved from the wreck." He was a chapel steward, a role which he took almost light-heartedly – until it came to auctioning off the flowers and vegetables from the Harvest Supper, at which he excelled.

If my mother wasn't on her knees in Chapel, she'd be on her knees in the garden, for gardening was her secular passion, and very good at it she was too. Grandfather Wyatt would sometimes offer to help out if he was passing – on condition that no-one told his wife, Sarah (Dinham as was), my Granny. For mother and mother-in-law did not get on. Even my God-fearing mother could not bring herself to love a near neighbour who played cards and drank gin, as Granny did, and the antipathy was mutual. Towards the end of her life, when she and my mother were living under the same roof, they would never sit at the same table. It almost goes without saying that they were on opposite sides of the Protestant divide. For my father's parents were C of E, worshipping regularly at Wiveliscombe's handsome parish church, travelling there by governess car drawn by the pony, Gypsy, who would be tied up to the railings outside the church and given a nosebag to keep him happy.

My father, on the other hand, was easy-going, not much good at business and dominated by my mother. He had inherited something of his mother's fondness for the good life, a tendency that would sometimes be revealed when the two of us were out together, at a rugby match or the cricket, and he would let his hair down and have a pint or two and occasionally even a cigarette. He was a good man and a decent, if old-fashioned, farmer, happy with his lot and not in any way ambitious or driven.

My first school was Wiveliscombe Primary, about a mile and a half away along the main road from Taunton to Barnstaple. I would walk there and back every day, usually meeting up with Freddie Horn, David Down and Marwood Osmond at Croford Bridge and then walking on together, in all weathers. At some stage I remember asking my father who the boys' fathers were. "They were all dug up under a gooseberry bush," he replied, before adding "although one of them was made on top of a load of hay!"

Luxuries may have been few and far between, but we were well fed. My father grew all of the family's vegetables, meat came weekly from the local butcher, topped up with the occasional rabbit, and groceries were delivered in vans from the County Stores in Wiveliscombe. I also remember a fish-man, in a pony and trap, shouting out "No fish today, only bloaters" as he drove past the farm.

My mother's parents farmed at Burchers Farm, not far across the fields from Edbrookes. It is north-facing and one of the steepest, most difficult farms in the area, a farm which my father used to say never saw sun by day or moon by night. But Grandfather Reed was the ideal man to take it on: meticulous, a perfectionist in everything he did. Whether it was making a hedge, building a rick or making a load, it was always a work of art. One of his more remarkable achievements came when he was working at Capton, when he cut the whole of the field that is now the Roadwater playing field, including the banks, with a scythe in a day.

I remember turning the grinding stone for him to sharpen shears, hooks and scythes, with me wondering if he would ever finish. He had a fine eye for a piece of ash and would select and cut out from his hedges the handles for his shovels, picks and scythes, keeping them in a barrel for whenever they were needed. But his pride and joy were his farm horses, which were always beautifully turned out. One of his great delights was to spend his evenings in their stables, polishing the horse-brasses to glittering perfection and all the time singing Methodist and Sankey hymns. Bill Stevens, who helped him out on the farm from time to time, always said that he wasted too much time on appearances. Of his perfectionism, he would say to me: "There goes your grandfather again, putting a shilling in and getting sixpence out."

As a Methodist farmer, my grandfather had no time for the tithe, the tax on farm output that was levied to fund the Anglican Church. I well remember him saying that he would never support the Church of England while putting money in the Methodist plate. By the 1930s it had become deeply unpopular and controversial, to the extent that there were anti-tithe marches and demonstrations, often with the involvement of Oswald Mosley's British Union of Fascists. Grandfather did go on one march in London, but it made no difference. When the time came for him to retire and sell the farm in 1941, all of the back tithe that he owed was bundled up and taken out of the proceeds of the farm sale. Grandfather was furious, blaming a combination of his bank manager and the auctioneer, but there was no escaping it. He and my grandmother retired to the cottage at the back of Edbrookes where I had ridden my tricycle, but the chunk that had been taken out of their retirement nest egg left them badly off. Grandfather put his gardening skills to good use around the neighbourhood, and there was always the chapel. But even that came to an end when the 'tortoise' stoves were replaced by electric heating, leaving grandfather to conclude, sadly, that "They clearly don't want me here, so I'm joining the Salvation Army."

My father had a bicycle, with a seat on the crossbar for me. A sheepdog called Blue Pup would sometimes accompany us on our jaunts. When we got to the cross-roads behind Hillacre, father would say 'keep off' to Blue Pup, who would race away to Ford, while father cycled furiously back to Edbrookes, hoping to beat Blue Pup back to home.

One other particularly vivid memory from my childhood is of an otter hunt. One morning I spotted a large group of men down by the Hillfarrance Brook, dressed in plus twos and armed with long poles. With these, they stabbed at the banks of the brook to flush out their quarry, with the hounds standing by. But the otter gave them the slip and passed close by where I was standing, in the field we now call Piggery, on his way to the mill stream which carried water to Croford Mill. I said nothing, while the otter disappeared, and the hunt headed off in the opposite direction towards Manor. It was a good day for the otter and a memorable day for me. I have never much liked hunting ever since.

Wiveliscombe's most famous family were the Hancocks. The family had lived in and around Wiveliscombe for centuries and were responsible for the town's most prominent landmark, the Hancocks' brewery, built by William Hancock in 1807. His son, another William, had ten sons, all mad keen on rugby, of whom two, Frank and Froude, played prominent parts in the early development of the game. Frank moved to Cardiff, to run the Hancocks brewery which had been opened in South Wales, and played rugby for Cardiff. He became captain of Wales, and he it was who devised what has become the accepted pattern of forwards and backs, by introducing what we now know as the three-quarter line. Froude, meanwhile, was making a name for himself playing for England and in 1891 for the first British Lions team on a tour of South Africa. In all, seven of the 10 Hancock brothers played rugby for Somerset and, of course, for Wiveliscombe RFC, which was founded in 1872 by Fred Rook, a Yorkshire-born engineer working on the Taunton to Barnstaple line.

I never met Froude Hancock, who died in 1933, but I do remember meeting Frank, usually on his horse in Castle Lane. The exchange that comes to mind would be opened by my father: "Good morning, Mr. Frank." "Good morning, Farmer Dick, and good morning, young man," after which they would chat about farming, the weather and whatnot. Frank's cousin, Willoughby, would become the President of Wiveliscombe Young Farmers' Club, when I was its Chairman, of which more anon.

One of the milestones in each farming year was threshing time, in the autumn. All of the local farmers used to help each other out. For example, I used to go to Burcher's or Fry's or Manor, and they would in turn reciprocate. King's the contractors would send a threshing machine powered by a steam traction engine called the Pride of Devon, which I'm glad to say is still going strong, with George and Wilf Routley, who came from Brompton Ralph, in attendance. They would arrive at around five o'clock to light the boiler and get the engine going, and my role was to make sure the boiler was kept topped up. To do this I had a grey mare called Blossom and a cart, carrying a hogshead barrel and a bucket. I'd drive this down to the river and dip the bucket into the river, climbing onto the shafts to tip the water into the barrel until it was full. Then I would drive back up to the farm, the engine would suck the water out of the barrel in no time and, before you knew it, they'd be on to me again: "More water, boy!"

The coming of war in 1939 brought big changes on the farm. It wasn't long before evacuees arrived from West Ham and Poplar in East London, mothers and children, their fathers having gone to war. We had Mrs Howitt and her two girls from Canvey Island at Edbrookes, while Granny Wyatt had Mrs Orford and her three boys at Hillacre. When the eldest, Bill, left school he came to work on the farm, driving the tractor. The children all went to school with the locals and mixed in pretty well, a few families remaining in Wiveliscombe after the war. I don't remember the name of the family who were billeted at Burchers, but I do remember Granny Reed picking nits out of their hair and treating them for the skin infection impetigo, which I then caught and still have the scars on my fingers 82 years later to show for it!

The war effort and the decrees of the all-powerful War Agricultural Executive Committee – commonly known as the 'WarAg' – made for some changes in cropping on the farm. Father grew flax, which I remember as being difficult to handle, pulled by a contractor's machine and sent to the flax mill at Lopen in South Somerset, and also sugar beet, which was sent by rail from Wiveliscombe station to the nearest factory at Kidderminster. Having a station nearby was a big asset in those days, especially as Wiveliscombe, unlike Milverton, had an elevated platform from which the trucks could readily be loaded. Besides the sugar beet, this came in handy for the wheat straw that we produced for thatching – wheat 'reed', as it is known – for dispatch to South Wales. After father and I and some of the station staff had loaded the trucks, we would push them under a measuring contraption, which was presumably set at the maximum height which would give the loaded truck clearance under the lowest bridge on the line. Our animal feed also came by rail. In fact, we must have been among the station's best customers, to the extent that the station-master would come over to the farm at Christmas-time to thank father for using the railway.

But the railway-related occasion which really stands out from those early days was when father walked a pedigree Devon bull, Croford Major, from the farm to the station. From there they travelled to Dulverton and the junction with the Exe Valley line, and so down to Exeter St David's. From there father walked his bull to the market, where Croford Major stood Reserve Champion at the Devon sale. It must have been a proud moment.

Father joined the Home Guard and became part of the Milverton company, which included Sgt Jack Loosemore and Lt Chris Shapland, father of Chris who would play a prominent part in my life in later years. But the man he went on duty with was Charlie Gadd, a neighbour. Each of the pair did two hours on and two hours off on the top of Croford Hill, looking out for fires and other incidents. Their down time was spent in Jack Loosemore's shepherd's hut, which was better than nothing but still meant little sleep for either of them, with a full day's work beckoning on the morrow. They never saw any German parachutists, although one morning my father did tell me that they'd seen two land mines dropped by parachute near Lydeard St Lawrence. Incendiary bombs were much more common and would be collected by some of the local children. The Germans were presumably trying to find Norton Manor camp – thankfully without success.

We were fortunate in never going short of meat during the war. Each family was allowed to kill two pigs a year which, at 400 lbs apiece (181 kilos) was more than enough to keep us all well fed, even if a lot of it was very fatty. Grandfather Reed killed and butchered the pigs, while family and friends made pies and salted the meat into a large salter in the dairy. It goes without saying that every bit of each pig was used, including the intestines, or chitterlings, which I can still see Granny Reed cleaning by the Hillfarrance Brook.

But we did lose our handsome iron railings against the road. They were taken to be melted down for the war effort but, as far as I'm aware, were never used. They're probably still in a quarry near Watchet or somewhere. Our neighbour across the way, Richard Bennett, was more cunning. He had paid the metal collectors to put his cast iron gate in a shed and, after the war, it was back in place. My mother was not amused.

3

Taunton School

Midway through the summer term of 1943 I was taken by my mother to meet Donald Crichton-Miller, the headmaster of Taunton School. Quite why she should have wanted to send me to Taunton School, rather than Queen's College, with its strong Methodist connections, I never knew, but I had done well at primary school in Wiveliscombe and was happy enough at the prospect.

Anyway, my first encounter with the formidable 'Crikey', as he was known, was an unforgettable experience. There were no introductions or pleasantries. Crichton-Miller simply pitched in with "I won't take him as a day boy." My mother, seemingly unperturbed, came back straightaway with "Right, headmaster, so will you take him as a boarder?" The answer must have been yes, because I started at Taunton School, in Winterstoke House, that autumn.

The boarding fees, modest though they seem now to have been at £30 a term, must have been a strain on my parents' limited resources, so it was just as well that I won a county scholarship. Included in this was my bus fare from Croford to Taunton on school days – a benefit which, as a boarder, I no longer needed. So my mother made the case to the County Education Department, supported by Crichton-Miller, that the money should go instead towards my boarding fees. After much correspondence, that small but important battle was lost.

Taunton School was a harsh place for an 11-year-old boy away from home for the first time. Every day began with a service in chapel, and as well as our lessons there was physical work to be done around the school. For this, every boy was assigned to a work squad, charged with gardening, cleaning or whatever. I was in the paper squad, with Roughtly, who became a bank manager in Minehead, and Weaver, who would join the County Gazette. We sorted and packed all sorts of paper, not helped by occasional visits from rats. A rather more

Winterstoke House, Taunton School, 1945

congenial occupation was growing potatoes on the headlands around the sports pitches and in the field which is now an all-weather hockey pitch. We were particularly keen on collecting ladybirds, just in case one of them turned out to be a Colorado beetle, for which the Ministry of Agriculture was offering a bounty!

I became a Scout soon after I arrived, joining Otter Patrol under the guidance of AA Smith, Assistant Housemaster of Winterstoke, and Mr Tewfik. Once a term we would pull a trek cart to the wood on the far side of Cothelstone Beacon up in the Quantocks and camp from Friday night to Sunday morning. On one such camp we saw a ghost – really – riding across the Beacon at midnight. In 1944 I graduated to the Cadet Corps, the nearest I ever got to the Army. Mr Tewfik was Egyptian and a good teacher who won the respect of his pupils. Goodness knows how Crikey came to employ him, but good teachers were hard to come by in wartime, as witnessed by the fact that we also had a German Jew on the staff, Mr Freudenberg.

Discipline was primitive. Once a fortnight we would have 'Form Master's Orders' when we would be lined up at the back of the classroom in order of performance. If you dropped three places from one order to the next, you would be put on a report card, and a bad report meant a caning from the headmaster. This was something I was fortunate enough to avoid, although I was beaten once: by AS Griffiths, who beat me with a cricket bat for some misdemeanour I was supposed to have committed whilst playing table tennis for Fairwater against Wills West house. But some of the punishments could be brutal. Years later I rang an Old Tauntonian England rugby international called David Hazell, to say that we were taking Crichton-Miller out to dinner to celebrate his 90th birthday and would he like to join us. "I don't want to see that old bastard again," was his reply. "I had to burn my pants before I went home to mother." Happily he did eventually relent and they ended up enjoying each other's company, as Crikey had been a Scottish international.

It was wartime, and one of my first experiences was air raid drill. There was a siren on a repository in Kingston Road which could clearly be heard from the school and, if it went off, we took our mattresses down to the main corridor and slept head to toe. That happened a number of times, fortunately with no harm done. We also had to practise our fire drill, which involved sliding down a canvas tube from a window on the top floor. It was scary but fun.

We shared the school with boys from two other schools which had been evacuated to Taunton, King's Rochester and Eltham College. Both had their own headmasters, so we not only had Crichton-Miller, known as 'The Monarch' to contend with but also the Rev 'The Devil' Davies, of Rochester and Occomore of Eltham. Both of the schools became houses and took part in all our sporting activities.

I soon settled down, making friends and shaking off any home-sickness. There was plenty of sport and any boy not participating in school or house games was required to go for a cross-country run. On Saturdays, if the school had a home match, we were all obliged to watch and cheer them on, which was no great hardship, as the standard of both rugby and cricket was high. The 1947 Taunton School First XV went through the entire season unbeaten, as well as winning the Richmond Sevens, and I was lucky enough to be able to watch David Sheppard, one of England's finest post-war batsmen and later Bishop of Liverpool, make a century for Sherborne on the Taunton ground. The worst thing about the school at that time was that law and order was mostly left in the hands of the prefects. Some, it is true, could be friendly and helpful, but others were little short of monsters. One of my early experiences at their hands was being dragged by the ear to the Prefects' Room and being made to stand outside while twelve prefects took turns at beating some unfortunate boy until he couldn't stand. The Head Boy would obviously have been complicit in that and other similar outrages. Many years later, at an Old Tauntonian function, I was introduced to the man who had been Head Boy in 1943. At the age of 86 it had taken him almost seventy years to pluck up the courage to come back to the school.

So I was pleased to relate what had happened to one of his successors, who must have been particularly unpopular. On his last day of school in 1947 he woke to find that all of his clothes had been stuffed into a sack and run up the school flagpole. In response, the entire school was made to stand in the parade ground until the culprit eventually owned up, many trains home having been missed in the interim. But that wasn't the end of it. The detested Head Boy was foolish enough to make a return visit to the school during the following term, when he was kidnapped by some of his victims, taken to the library, stripped and had 'Lending Library' stamped all over his body. As a final indignity he was thrown out naked into Cyril Street, with his clothes chucked after him. Boys could be brutal in those days as well!

4

A young farmer

Grandfather Wyatt had a stroke in Wiveliscombe market in 1941, from which he never recovered, spending the last five years of his life bed-ridden at Hillacre. He died in 1946, leaving Granny Wyatt to live on the ground floor in Hillacre with Auntie Mar, whilst we moved upstairs. But there was a surprise in his will. He had left the farm to me, giving my father only a lifetime's interest in it. I never quite understood why he'd done this. It might have been my Granny's influence, as I'd always got on very well with her, and there were even rumours that he'd left me the farm to keep me out of the Methodist pulpit, which was undoubtedly what my mother would have liked for me. At any rate, whatever the reason, it rankled with father.

In the summer term of 1948, in the midst of taking my School Certificate, I received a letter from him – the only letter he ever wrote me – to say "if you want to inherit the farm, you had better leave school and come and help me."

What to do? I was enjoying school and doing well, but there was no-one to turn to for advice. I didn't have any very clear idea of what I wanted to do by way of a career; probably something to do with agriculture, auctioneering maybe or train as a vet? In the end it seemed to me that I didn't have much choice but to go back to the farm and make the best of it. My mother wasn't particularly sympathetic or helpful, especially when she discovered that I'd got good grades in all my exam papers – except divinity!

The summer of 1948 was one of the hottest on record. The first task my father gave me was to cut back all of the many hedges on our 100 or so acres, armed only with a staff hook. Tormented by flies, my arms aching, my hands a mass of blisters, many was the time I wished myself back at school. All this, so that there was room for my father to clear the first few rows of barley up against each hedge with a scythe, before going in with the reaper-binder – horse-drawn if he was on board, tractor-drawn if it was my turn – using the Fordson tractor which we'd bought for something like £175 back in 1941 and which father never used.

All of this hard manual labour left plenty of time for me to think about my situation. It soon became clear to me that there was no future for two families on a 100-acre beef and arable farm. I needed my own enterprise, separate from the land. Something like a reasonably intensive pig unit. I'd met Tom Jefford, the manager of Lloyds Bank in Wiveliscombe, so decided to go and see him to talk it through. He thought the idea was a sound one and offered to lend me £200 (about £5,000 in present-day values).

My father was furious, having never borrowed a penny from anyone in his life. It seemed a betrayal of all that he stood for in business, something which he was never much good at. We used the money to buy some outdoor huts, and I started breeding pedigree Wessex Saddlebacks, which I enjoyed but which didn't make much commercial sense. We soon discovered that, in order to make a worthwhile amount of money, we needed to move into hybrid breeding, producing bacon pigs from about 50 sows.

The row over borrowing money prompted my father to step back. It was as if he was saying to me, "OK, if you want to do that sort of thing without even asking me first, you had better get on with it." So, at the age of 18, I was effectively the boss. There was no formal handover, although we did go to the family solicitor, Mr Couch of Moger and Couch in Wiveliscombe, to discuss a formal arrangement, but he advised against, presumably because he felt I was too young and inexperienced. In practice, though, all the decisions were made by me. Father was supportive, but he was a 'worker-at' rather than a planner for the future. The experience brought home to me the extent to which my mother was the driving force in the family. I often wonder what would have happened to me if she hadn't arranged for me to be given a good education.

The farm that I had effectively taken over was nominally 100 acres, but 10 per cent of that was cider orchard, the apples going to the Hancocks cider factory, another 10 per cent was growing hay for the farm horses, 10 per cent was bog and wasteland and then there were all the hedges. Probably only about half of the farm was growing crops for sale, mostly barley for Hancocks brewery. I well remember, every harvest, taking samples of our malting barley up to the brewery for Willoughby Hancock's inspection. He would summon his maltster and ask him what he thought of it. "Not much," he would usually reply. "I'll give you 120 shillings for every two sacks (£6 for four cwt, so £30/ton), and if you don't like it, you can always try selling it at Taunton Market." Which we never did, unlike Grandfather Reed, who, good Methodist that he was, wouldn't sell his barley to the brewery as a matter of principle. Instead he sold it to Smalls, a small-time grain merchant, who as often as not would then tell him to deliver it to the brewery. He would take it as far as the edge of town, but someone else had to haul it up to the brewery, lest Grandfather Reed's nostrils were assailed by the smell of the demon drink!

When it came to advice, I got most of it down the pub, the White Hart in Milverton, Fishers as it was known then, where some of the local farmers would gather every Monday evening, men like Tom Cottrell, Donald Farley, Charlie Burroughs and Jim Cottrell. These

Donald and Kath Farley, Gladys and Tom Cottrell

were experienced, successful farmers, and I gleaned everything I could from talking to them and listening to them. Mind you, it did lead to a lot of drinking! Like many a son from a teetotal family – and I'd even been made to take the pledge! – I took to it like a duck to water. We drank beer up to turn-out time and whisky afterwards. Many was the time when I came out of Fishers at four o'clock in the morning, sometimes to be visited by the police to check my movement book the following morning. On one such occasion the policeman said to me, "You were late last night." I said, "Yes, that's true enough, but I didn't see you on my way home." But they'd seen me! What my mother would have made of all of this had she known about it, I dread to think.

My other social activities at this stage mostly revolved around the Wiveliscombe Young Farmers Club. I'd joined straightaway after leaving school and became an active member, taking part in all the competitions I could. This taught me a lot as well, about stock-judging, ploughing, gate-making, hedge-laying and so on. There were all sorts of practical things going on, often involving competitions with other clubs. I was part of the quiz team that won the County Cup and of the similarly successful public speaking team.

In 1951 I was elected Chairman of Wiveliscombe Young Farmers' Club. One of the first duties of an incoming Chairman was to have a meeting with the President, Mr Willoughby Hancock. At our meeting he told me that there would be two dances at the cider factory and that he would arrange for a doorkeeper, a barman and a lady to deal with the elsan closets. After both dances I was summoned to meet Mr Willoughby.

On the first occasion, he said to me: "We're in trouble, Wyatt. The elsans were emptied onto a row of runner beans." After some discussion he said something to the effect of "Oh don't worry, Wyatt. Leave it to me. I'll sort it, and in the meantime go to Inder in wines and spirits and take a bottle of gin for your grandmother." Each time I saw Mr Willoughby I left with a bottle of gin for granny.

Following the second dance I was again summoned to see him. "We are in more trouble, Wyatt," he began. "Bill Pulsford is complaining about French letters left on his hay, which was in a shed opposite the primary school." But again he said he'd sort it, and granny got her bottle of gin!

Young Farmers Public Speaking Competition
Victoria Rooms, Milverton, 3 February 1951
Les Hill, Ron Greenway, Wesley Wyatt, Audrey Brown

The YFC's reputation as a marriage bureau for the countryside was entirely deserved. It wasn't sometimes known as 'the young fathers' club' for nothing! Relationships were made, broken, became marriages and occasionally ended in divorce. It was at a Young Farmers dance that I met my first wife, Evelyn Gibbons, always known as Mary. We hit it off straightaway, as she had just left school at Weirfield School for Girls, Taunton School's near neighbour across Staplegrove Road.

Wiveliscombe Market was the centre of local agricultural activity in those days. On the third Tuesday of each month, cattle and sheep would be walked into market from the surrounding farms. In the busiest spring months, the animals would be held in the street until space was available in the market. The railway also played an important part, with cattle trucks standing ready to transport stock for away buyers and dealers.

My first professional visit to the market involved selling a heifer. She was a good heifer, but bidding stopped when she reached £35, when I had vowed to myself not to sell her for less than £40 and said so. No sooner had I spoken than at least six dealers – one of whom turned out to be my future father-in-law - said, "Book her to me"!

During and after the Second World War, the market was also a grading centre where a local butcher and a local farmer graded animals on behalf of the Ministry of Food. In the late 1950s, when my mother and father were away in Canada with cousin Hector on their first ever holiday, I walked the sheep, which had been grazing on roots, to the market. "Take them home, boy," said the graders. "They're not fat enough!"

Market Committee meetings were interesting occasions. They were held in the brewery offices at 6pm under the chairmanship of Mr Willoughby Hancock who, at 7 o'clock, whatever stage the proceedings had reached, would declare the meeting closed, with the words "Enjoy yourselves, gentlemen, and leave us to much refreshment." Whatever remained to be decided would then be sorted out by Frank Morle or Arthur Tarr, the local auctioneers.

In the 1950s I also became a regular at Taunton Market on a Saturday morning, particularly during the winters. I met many good and interesting farmers there, including JC 'Farmer' White, who played 15 Test matches for England, mostly from 1928 to '31, captaining them twice, and who took 2,165 wickets for Somerset with his slow left arm, more than any other bowler in the county's history. Not that you would guess any of that from meeting him. He was friendly, polite and modest, but quiet to the point of taciturnity. They say he was a considerable poker player in the Somerset dressing room when the rain came down and the cards came out, and I can well believe it. He was a man who gave nothing away, both on the cricket pitch and off it. Much later, in the 1970s, I played golf with his son Tom and also knew his daughter Norah. They too were understated and never used their father's fame and reputation to promote themselves.

5

George

One day in the early 1960s, out of the blue, I received a telephone call from my cousin Ruth Branfield, who was nursing at Musgrove Park Hospital in Taunton. She asked me to put her through to my mother, but would I stay on the line. She said that a 'black man' had arrived, hoping to go to college and train as a nurse, but had nowhere to stay. Could we help? My mother hesitated for a moment but, no doubt recalling the Second Commandment, then said 'Bring him over so we can meet him.'

Father, George and Mother
outside Hillacre farmhouse

It turned out that the man in question was Niell Musheba Logovani. He came from a large cattle-owning family in rural Kenya and had been desperate to come to England to further his education. A letter sent from his Catholic missionary school, addressed simply to 'The Educational

41

Officer, England', had remarkably made its way to the right official quarter, and George had been offered a place at the Somerset Technical College, provided he could raise enough money for his air fare. Thanks to a reluctant gift of 20 cows from his father, the money was raised and George arrived, although how he ended up at Musgrove we never did discover.

But mother and father decided to take him in, and he soon became one of the family, calling my mother 'The Mother', and my father 'The Father'. Despite, or perhaps because of, his colour, he fitted in well, making friends wherever he went and – for black men were a distinct rarity in West Somerset in the 1960s – becoming something of a local celebrity. He was also more than useful around the farm, helping out with the pigs and doing odd jobs whenever he had time off.

With the potato harvester
Bob Graham, George, Ivy Redwood and Christine Venton

Having passed his nursing exams he left Musgrove and decided he wanted to join the Royal Army Medical Corps. This proved to be easier said than done but, after some intervention by myself and my parents, it was arranged that he should meet an RAMC Colonel in Taunton, and that did the trick. For the next 20 years or so, he served in Singapore where he first encountered Sir John Harding, Tidworth in Wiltshire, Winchester, Isolhon in West Germany and then Brecon. He always kept in touch and would visit us when he was on leave. So we were naturally worried when we heard nothing from him for some ten months. I made some inquiries and from what I could gather, George couldn't come on leave because he was too busy undertaking other soldiers' duties. Using my political connections, I decided to raise this with Edward du Cann when we were out canvassing together. Two days later George appeared, his first words being "Please don't report me to the War Office."

It was whilst he was at Brecon that he arranged for two of his nieces, Mitume and Ajema, to be educated at the Ursuline Convent in Brecon. Major Sutton, George's commanding officer, would ring me from time to time to discuss his progress. I asked him how on earth was George going to be able to afford the school fees. "God knows," he replied. And God probably did know, because it soon became clear that the Catholic Church was helping out, through the convent.

The two girls often came to visit us at Croford, always dressed in smart school uniform. Yet when they had arrived in Britain they had no European clothing. George saw to that, just as he did to everything else involved with their welfare.

Ajume and Mitume

In time George became one of the longest serving private soldiers in the British army, before eventually being promoted to lance-corporal in 1984 and assigned to look after the by now Field Marshal The Lord Harding, former Chief of the General Staff, who had been his commanding office in Singapore, who had broken his hip and was in hospital in Yeovil.

When Lord Harding had recovered sufficiently to be allowed back to his home at Nether Compton, George went with him. Olive and I visited one evening to collect George and take him out to supper in Sherborne. Lord Harding, sitting by a life-size portrait of himself, asked George to fetch me a glass of whisky. Whilst he was away, Harding confided in me, "George is a wonderful chap, but he is bloody useless at pouring whisky!" Lord Harding was by no means the only member of the great and the good to be on first-name terms with George. When Field Marshal Lord Bramall arrived at Nether Compton, it was to see George as well as Lord Harding, and the Queen Mother was another visitor whom George seems to have got to know.

One morning in January 1989, I had a phone call from George. "Lord Harding is dead," he said. "Where is he?" I asked. "In my arms," he replied.

Before he died, Lord Harding must have arranged for George to take his nieces to Nairobi to see their mother, the widow of one of his many brothers. This he did in the spring of 1989. About two weeks after they left, I received a telephone call from a solicitor in Yeovil to say that George had died and that I was the sole trustee of his estate. The girls returned not long afterwards, with a sad tale to tell. George had been murdered by his extended family because he would not give them the money he had ear-marked for the girls' education. It was a tragic end to a remarkable life dedicated to education, service and his fellow man.

Happily that did not go unrecognised. In the 1989 Queen's Birthday Honours, George was awarded, posthumously, the British Empire Medal. The following year, a call came from the Army to say that they were arranging an investiture at the Convent in Brecon to present the two girls with George's BEM and a long service medal, and would I speak at the event? I needed no second bidding.

So, in July 1990, cousin Ruth, daughter Jayne, Olive and myself drove to Brecon where we had lunch at the Wellington Hotel with Field Marshal Lord Bramall, another former Chief of the General Staff, who would be conducting the investiture. Towards the end of what was a thoroughly enjoyable meal, Lord Bramall turned to me and asked me, quietly, who was paying for the food. Remembering that he had recently been President of the MCC, I told him that I would pay, provided he sent me some Test match tickets. Almost by return, they arrived, for the Lord's Test against India, where we saw David Gower score a cameo 40 and Graham Gooch a monumental, if sometimes a bit dull, 333.

Security was tight in Brecon, given the threat from the IRA, and Lord Bramall told me that all of the occupants of the rooms in the Wellington had been checked to make sure they were who they said they were, and that one room appeared to have been booked under an assumed name. The security men had duly broken into the room, only to find a presumably unmarried couple enjoying a spot of midday nookie!

Lord Bramall, Olive and me at Brecon

Lord Bramall spoke with real feeling at the Investiture, telling us all that if the phone went late at night it would almost certainly be George, calling to inquire as to his welfare. A lowly Lance Corporal ringing the Chief of the General Staff! It showed the esteem in which George was held, as did the fact that not long afterwards I had a letter from the Queen Mother's private secretary, asking that HM be kept informed of the progress of George's nieces. So their school reports were duly sent off to Clarence House, a letter of thanks from the Queen Mother invariably arriving soon afterwards.

Some years later, Olive and I were on holiday in Nairobi, staying at the Norfolk Hotel. We knew that Mitume wanted to make a career in the tourism industry, so I asked the hotel manager if there was any chance of her being given a job. He said that there was, prompting me to add that if he wanted a further reference, I was sure that Sir Edward Du Cann would be happy to provide it. Big mistake! "I wish you hadn't mentioned that name," the manager replied. It turned out that the hotel was owned by Tiny Rowland, with whom Du Cann was much involved and who was evidently not thought very highly of!

When Mitume had finished her schooling we put her on a plane to Nairobi and waited for news of her progress. After about ten days we had a phone call from the hotel manager, to say that Mitume was everything that we had promised, but that she couldn't speak Swahili, so would need further education. I thought long and hard about what best to do when a thought suddenly came to me. David Evans, an Old Tauntonian whom I had known well, was running an import-export business in Nairobi. I called him and he answered the phone. "Good morning, David," I said. There was a pause, and then the reply, "Good morning, Gaffer" – Gaffer having been my nickname at school – "What can I do for you?"

He could not have been more helpful, taking Mitume out of the Norfolk Hotel, arranging the education she needed and eventually giving both of the girls jobs in his business. What a friend! Sadly, we lost touch with the girls following numerous begging letters from their mother. Even more sadly, we also lost David from cancer. Part of his treatment was at Addenbrooke's Hospital in Cambridge, where I was able to visit him, to thank him and talk about the old days. Despite his suffering, they were fun times.

6

Family farmer

Mary and I got married in 1955, in Bampton, where her father farmed. My best man was Rob Venner, the father of the auctioneer Robert Venner of Greenslade Taylor Hunt, and the church was full of Young Farmers, celebrating the union of yet another pair of 'their own'. We set up home at Hillacre, mother and father having moved into the bungalow they'd built, called Shells, behind the farmhouse.

Mary set about deep litter poultry and started what proved later to be a very successful bed-and-breakfast business. I, meanwhile, was busy modernising the farm, taking out hedges, straightening the Hillfarrance Brook and draining the wetter land. I even bulldozed the cider orchard, all of this environmental devastation, as it would be regarded nowadays, generously supported by Ministry of Agriculture grants.

Reggie Westcott removing the stumps of the apple trees

Straightening Hillfarrance Brook

My son Robert was born in 1958, with Jayne following in 1959. Soon afterwards, my in-laws, the Gibbons family, decided to move from Bampton to be nearer Mary and bought Millands farm, which adjoined both Hillacre and Croford. This was maybe not an entirely happy arrangement, but I did have the consolation of being able to farm the land (and remove some of the hedges on it!).

Hillacre farm was a very happy place when the children were growing up, thanks not least to Mary, who was the heart and soul of the household. To give an idea of how much she contributed to our family, I can do no better than to quote part of the tribute which Jayne paid to her mother at her funeral in 2019:

> If you knew her either through the farm, or through her love
> of sport, or because you had stayed at the farm for b-and-b,
> or maybe lodged there, or even if you just lived nearby, she
> will have been your friend. Hard work was mum's life. It was
> what she enjoyed and was happy being the director of her own
> farmhouse b-and-b. She did cricket teas, she picked potatoes,
> she kept poultry, she made the best clotted cream, she prepared

and delivered meals on wheels to the lads working on the land, and, on top of all this, scrubbing floors, cleaning windows and keeping everything spick and span. Preparing cooked breakfast or a three-course meal for guests didn't faze her. It was what she loved.

Robert and I had the happiest time as kids growing up on the farm. There was always something happening and people about. When we started school our friends were always encouraged to visit, and there was lots of excitement and laughter.

Hillacre was, obviously, somewhere that people liked to be. If they came once, they came back. Paying guests became friends. It was a place where everyone was welcome, and there were always teas with homemade cakes and biscuits. Mum was a real home-maker and an excellent cook.

At Christmas anyone locally who had nowhere to go was invited to Hillacre. If they were too elderly or infirm to come to us, then Christmas dinner was delivered to their homes. Sunday lunch was a ritual and it didn't matter who happened to be about. There was always enough and they were invited. Mum just had a unique way of making people feel welcome.

That was indeed a happy time, although just occasionally the fun and games would misfire, such as the occasion when Jayne and Robert locked themselves in an upstairs cupboard and were only rescued when Shirley, our live-in help, heard Jayne's cries for help, by which time her fingers were raw from trying to scratch at the door to get it open.

I'm sure this experience contributed to the claustrophobia and nerves that Jayne suffered from subsequently, conditions that were not helped in any way by two occasions when we found ourselves entertaining unwelcome visitors. The first of these involved a loud knocking at the door at two o'clock in the morning. I went down the stairs to find out what was up, with Jayne shouting after me, "Don't let them in, Dad."

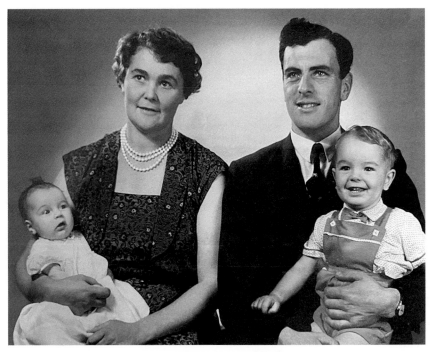

Jayne, Mary, me and Robert

On opening the door I discovered a man, obviously agitated and frightened, who burst past me, saying, "Lock the door, Wes. I'm not leaving here without police protection." It turned out to be a local man called Desmond Green, who had armed himself with a bent poker and appeared to have reached the farmhouse via the river. I sat him down, rang the police and gave him some coffee, and we were joined in no time by our local copper, Fred Smith, who also had a cup of coffee and didn't seem at all bothered. It appeared that there had been some local fracas involving Desmond, which Fred clearly thought would blow over.

On the second occasion I was awoken by an intruder who, upon being challenged, said that he had seen a light on and thought we were open, presumably for bed and breakfast. Again I rang the police and gave them a description of our visitor, who was also by now enjoying a cup of coffee. "Oh we know him," they said. "He's only recently been in the station." And before very long, they arrived to collect him – much to Jayne's relief. There were tears shed when we sent Robert to

Connaught House School in Bishop's Lydeard, even more tears when he went to Taunton School as a boarder, and floods of tears when I suggested that he should take up a farm apprenticeship with Alexander Simpson Ltd, in faraway Tibberrmore near Perth in Scotland, who supplied us with seed potatoes.

Jayne went to Bishop Fox's School in Taunton, after which she took a catering course at the local technical college. When she left college she asked me what she should do next. I said, "Apply for the jobs which are advertised." She took me at my word and almost immediately applied, with 59 others, for a job manning the AA portacabin at the Taunton Deane Services on the M5, which had recently been opened. She was offered the job but couldn't see what it had got to do with catering. I reminded her of the scope of the AA's activities and the opportunities which they offered – of which, in time, she took full advantage, becoming a bed-and-breakfast inspector, a hotel inspector and, eventually, the leader of the AA's entire team of hotel inspectors.

Robert was never particularly academic but he was a fine all-round sportsman, both at Connaught House School, Bishop's Lydeard and later when he followed me to Taunton School. One sportsday at Connaught House I asked him how many events he hoped to win. Modestly he said he hoped to come second in most of them. Competitive chap that I am, this didn't particularly impress me, so I stood next to the running track and yelled at him. He won all the races!

Robert went on to marry Clare Connell and they had two boys, James and Tom. James is now working in the timber business, while Tom has inherited his father's sporting prowess and is a professional rugby union player, on the books of Exeter Chiefs and, at the time of writing, on loan to the Cornish Pirates. My third grandson is Hugh, the product of a brief liaison between between Robert and Lara Moore, but none the less loved for that and very much part of the family."

But back to the farm. In 1963, on a Saturday evening in the White Hart, Tom Cottrell, whom I always knew as 'Uncle Tom', asked me, "Who bought the farm?" I had no idea what farm he was talking about and said so. "Brewers Farm, Fitzhead," he replied. A bit later Donald Farley arrived and was asked exactly the same question. "It wasn't sold," he replied.

"You buy that farm Monday morning, boy," said Tom, in a tone that would brook no argument. Which I did, the only problem being, as it turned out, that I had to rely on father-in-law for a lot of the finance, something that would eventually come back to haunt me.

Brewers was 108 acres, with a new house, for all of which we paid £17,000. With Hillacre, it meant that I was farming over 200 acres – on my own. What with the demands of the farm, and of a young family, it meant that I was working every hour that God gave and then some. The strain of this was brought home to me one day in the spring of 1964 when I'd been up all night ploughing at Brewers to get the ground fit for spring barley. Jack Loosemore stopped me on my way home at seven o'clock in the morning, discovered I'd been up all night, told me I was mad and said that he was going to send help. Before long, we were growing potatoes together, an arrangement that, with the recruitment of Chris Shapland of Dene Farm, Fitzhead and Martin White of Blagroves and considerable assistance from the Central Council for Agricultural and Horticultural Co-operation (CCAHC) became Deane Growers. Between us we grew 100 acres of potatoes. Thanks not least to the efforts of ADAS's Tony Lester-Card, grants were forthcoming for feasibility studies, machinery and buildings, and our joint venture was soon a roaring success. So much so that we discussed expanding the group to take in arable farmers to the east of Taunton like Peter Parris, John Vile and Robin Leaney, although the county town itself proved too big an obstacle and they eventually went their own way as Wyvern Farms.

One of the advantages of pooling our potato-growing efforts was that we could use contractors at harvest time. Chris Summers, a local farmer, did the organising, effectively becoming what we would now know as a 'gangmaster', even if his workers were distinctly local: Christine Venton whose husband worked for Chris Shapland, Eileen the wife of our shepherd John Smith, Margaret and Robert Walton from Knights as well as several women from Milverton. The harvester itself came from Mountfield Farm Contractors.

But while the potato business was profitable, I'm not sure it did the land much good. In wet autumns, of which there were plenty, the harvester and the potato trailers were forever getting bogged down

Deane Growers
Jack Loosemore, Wesley Wyatt, Martin White, Chris Shapland, Keith Keyte

One hundred acres of potatoes

and churning up the soil. Stone removal was another big issue, first by hand, later mechanically. There were times when it seemed more like an exercise in removing potatoes from stones, rather than stones for potatoes, and it greatly increased the risk of soil erosion, especially from sloping fields. I've got few regrets about the way I have farmed over the years, but growing potatoes and the attendant damage to soil structure is certainly one of them.

Meanwhile, I still had the pig unit and decided that, with everything else I was trying to cope with, I needed a good pigman to ease the load. I'd heard that there was a man in Milverton, Jack Julian, who was looking for work. When he came to see me I was impressed and engaged him. He had been farming at Skilgate, the other side of Wiveliscombe, but had somehow got involved with an unscrupulous money-lender and had lost his business. Jack turned out to be one of the most caring stockmen I ever knew. He became so attached to the pigs that when the lorry arrived to take pigs to the abattoir, Jack would make himself scarce. But he was pretty hopeless when it came to money. He and his wife were by now living with his father-in-law, who seemed to be almost as bad as the money-lender. He had made Jack bankrupt and was taking all his earnings, leaving him with only enough money for the bus fare to Hillacre. When I discovered what was going on, I was shocked and made up my mind, with Jack's agreement, to have the bankruptcy removed.

After completing any number of forms we eventually got a date for a court hearing in Taunton. This turned out to be quite an experience. I sat at the back of the court next to Tiny Weaver, a rather large retired policeman, while poor Jack was being cross-examined about his business dealings, including his job looking after my pigs. Jack was nervous and flustered by the interrogation, and I could sense the judge becoming more and more impatient and exasperated with him.

"This isn't fair," I said to Tiny Weaver.

"Well then, stand up and say so," he replied.

So up I stood. Seeing me, the judge sent one of the clerks to find out what was going on and told me to sit down. But it did the trick. I was summoned to the front of the court to explain myself and told the judge all about Jack's honesty and decency but also his vulnerability, particularly to unscrupulous money-lenders and controlling fathers-in-law. When I'd finished, the judge said, "Clear the court; bankruptcy will end in 60 days." We'd won!

Tiny Weaver shook me by the hand and said well done, and the Somerset County Gazette carried a report on the case under the headline: "Farmer tells court his worker too good to be bankrupt." Jack Julian could not have been happier.

By the autumn of 1967 I had been growing continuous barley for four years. With every year yields dropped, from a respectable two tons per acre in 1964 to a dismal one and a quarter tons in 1967. I knew what was needed to turn things around: livestock and specifically sheep – the old 'golden hoof'. So I said to father, "I'm going to Wales, would you like to come?"

"What on earth do you want to go to Wales for?" he asked.

"To buy sheep," I replied.

We went to McCartneys auction in Knighton and bought Kerry Hill and Beulah two-tooth ewes. One of the first purchases was from Ifor Williams who at the time were in the process of building the first of their legendary livestock trailers. We bought 50 ewes in all, which were sent to Wiveliscombe station by rail, arriving the next day in a livestock van on the back of the one o'clock train from Taunton to Barnstaple. There the wagon was put in a siding to await the arrival of father, me, a sheep dog and our bicycles, to be walked home along the main road to Croford.

In 1967 Davy's Farm, now known as Croford House, came up for sale. It adjoined Hillacre so was an obvious opportunity for further expansion. I collected my mentor, Uncle Tom, and we looked from the road at some old buildings, half-buried in nettles, and the 56 acres included in the sale. I remember saying to him, "Well, what can be done with that?" To which he replied, "You buy it, boy. You'll do something with it."

The first thing I did was to run a telephone auction with Joe Leigh-Firbank, of Manor Farm on the main road into Wiveliscombe, who wanted it for his eldest son, Roger. I managed in the end to outbid him but still needed to raise the money. As before, I went to see my bank manager at Lloyds in Wiveliscombe, who by now was a Mr Bell. When I explained what I was about, he almost exploded: "Buy a farm?! Buy a farm?! Don't you know there's a bloody credit squeeze on?"

Undeterred, I went across the road to the wine and spirit merchants Applegates and bought the biggest bottle of gin in the shop. This I carried back to Mr Bell and told him that I still wanted to buy a farm. We talked it through at length, and eventually he came up with an offer. The bank would lend me the money, provided I sold off the house and six acres, which I did, for £6,500. That house, largely untouched, was sold not long ago for £880,000! Anyway, I had acquired 50 acres of good land for £11,000, or £220 an acre. It was a lot more than the £158/acre I had paid for Brewers just four years earlier and that had included a new house. But even so, I was happy with my purchase and, if a lot of people said at the time that I was going too fast and over-stretching myself, I was saved by inflation.

It was in 1970, at a Deane Growers meeting, that Chris Shapland suggested we should consider merging our entire farming businesses so as to avoid all the paperwork involved in recording hours of works and other contributions to the potato business. Martin White and Jack Loosemore weren't keen on the idea, so Chris and I decided to go it alone and merge our various enterprises – barring potatoes, which would stay with Deane Growers – to form Fitzhead Farms.

We valued our various assets with the help of the auctioneer, Ted Sharland, and decided to write off major investments over ten years, so that if the business folded, everything would have a price and massive expenditure on lawyers could be avoided.

Working with Chris as Fitzhead Farms was the high point of my farming career. Bringing our farms together meant that we were farming an economic unit of around 550 acres, could afford to recruit a top quality workforce and could each concentrate on our strengths. Chris looked after the beef and the arable, and I looked after the pigs and sheep. There was no plan as such. The business just seemed to evolve naturally. We worked well together, making decisions as we went along and taking expert advice when it came to the really big investments, like the new pig unit.

It helped that Chris was the sort of man it was impossible not to get along with. At a quarter to one every day, no matter what we were doing, he would stop work and set off to drive two or three local people to the pub and buy them a drink. That's the sort of man he was. He was a putter-together, not a taker-apart. It was he who led the way on our conservation work, like re-planting hedges and planting trees along the old railway line. The Farming and Wildlife Advisory Group (FWAG) was formed in the 1980s, Somerset being one of the first branches, with Chris as its Chairman, so his influence stretched far beyond our corner of West Somerset. Sadly he died much too young.

The new business was an almost immediate success. The amount of production we were achieving was phenomenal, and it wasn't long before we decided that we needed more skilled labour, specifically a pig manager and a head shepherd. We recruited John Thompson to run the pig unit, of whom more anon, and, after a good deal of gentle persuasion from myself, John Smith as head shepherd. Both turned out to be exceptional managers, with John Smith becoming runner-up in the national Shepherd of the Year competition in 1980. As so often in farming, it was his attention to detail which made him such an outstanding shepherd.

John Smith

At work with the sheep

When John and his family arrived at Brewers in 1975 we were planning a new sheep shed at Dene, next door to the Deane Potatoes store which we had built. The aim was to be able to lamb 1500 ewes indoors, out of the wind and rain. Phillips of Hereford were given the contract to build it, and it was big, so big that it soon became the talk of the locality. In January 1978 we were persuaded to hold an open day so that other farmers could see what we were up to and could learn from it. The ewes had all been shorn before going into the shed in November and were looking in fine condition, with a lambing percentage of around 200 confidently expected.

How often does pride come before a fall! Disaster struck in March when a blizzard swept across Somerset and eight feet of snow was blown onto one corner of the shed, which collapsed, the massive steel uprights twisted like matchwood. Arthur Venton, who lived opposite, phoned me to tell me what had happened, something I found difficult to believe. I drove a tractor to the top of Croford Hill and then walked across Donald Farley's fields to get to the Top Way and the shed. What greeted me when I got there was a horrible, shattering sight.

A horrible sight

But there was no time for tears or reflection. The first task was to put a number of badly injured ewes out of their misery. I went home and rang the vet, Gordon Bridges, who said I could borrow his humane killer. So I drove the tractor into Wilscombe to pick it up, went back to the shed and then killed 50 ewes, all carrying twins. It was undoubtedly the worst moment in my farming life.

The good people of Fitzhead could not have been more supportive or concerned and came to help in whatever way they could. And once the roads had been cleared we had other visitors – the loss adjusters arriving in big cars with their building consultants in tow and, as news spread, the media. All the BBC reporter seemed to want to know was whether my losses were covered by insurance. My reply wasn't terribly polite, but I think I made my point – that the only thing that mattered to me was the welfare of my sheep, and would they and the other reporters please leave us in peace so that we could get on with the business of lambing, which was just getting under way.

Once the initial fuss had died down, it struck me that I hadn't seen the under-shepherd, Reg Larcombe, for at least two weeks. When I eventually went to his home to ask him what was going on, I found him sitting in front of the fire. He told me he was looking after the neighbours. Stressed and tired as I was, this was too much. I knew that his wife had been a big help to Chris Shapland after the loss of his wife Lois, but even so, this was not to be borne, so I sacked him on the spot.

This did not work out well. Some months later, the farm workers' union became involved and I ended up in an Industrial Tribunal in Exeter, where we lost, although I shall always believe that what I did, whilst certainly headstrong, was fully justified under the circumstances.

By this stage we had switched from buying replacement ewes at Knighton, to buying ewe lambs bred by Jack Anderson and family at Cambo in Northumberland. John and I had been impressed by his sheep when we had visited the farm on a Southern Counties Sheep Group tour, and they turned out to be every bit as good as we'd hoped. From then on, every year, Jack would phone me on the first Friday in August to tell me the price of similar lambs sold at Scots Gap market that day. After agreeing numbers and price, he would always ask me if I "minded a bit of horn", the reason being that the lambs were from Scotch Blackface mothers and Blueface Leicester rams. It didn't bother me particularly but one year, knowing that Jack was concerned about head fly, which was associated with horned animals, I suggested he use a Gritstone ram to breed the horns out. He tried it but the following year he said he didn't like the 'lugs', ears in other words, on the resultant lambs. They looked all right to me, but evidently not to Jack, even though the shape of the 'lugs' could have no bearing whatsoever on the quality of the meat!

My happy association with Jack and his family over many years came to a sad conclusion. He died in his sheep shed of a heart attack in 2000, and when Olive and I travelled north the following year to visit his widow and family we found a roomful of people in utter despair. The lifetime's work of the Anderson family had been wiped out by foot-and-mouth disease. It was a scene of wretchedness that has stayed with me ever since.

Back in 1975 we were looking to recruit a pig manager as well as a head shepherd. At a Banjo Potatoes meeting in Exeter, I mentioned this to Peter Findlay, a lecturer at Bicton College of Agriculture. He said he had just the student for our needs. So not long afterwards, I went to Bicton to meet John Thompson. My first words to him, as he subsequently never ceased to remind me, were: "You're late!" But after that unpromising beginning, John and I got on famously and he came to Hillacre to expand the unit.

From a modest 50 sows, we planned to expand the herd to 250. We discussed buildings with a number of suppliers before deciding on a Belgian firm, Lambert Geerkens. Chris Shapland, John, our vet Gordon Bridges and myself flew to Antwerp to meet Mr Geerkens, who drove us to the factory Weg op Bree near the German border. It was an unforgettable day, with ideas and drawings being sent to his draughtsmen in the next room, which we could adjust however we pleased. In the end we ordered sow housing, farrowing housing and fattening buildings, all to be delivered to Hillacre for erection by Cliff Smoldon, our local builder.

On the day when the first load was due, I sent a message to Mr Geerkens to say that the driver would need to be aware of the one-way system outside the farm and would need to stop in the lay-by opposite until I fetched him. On the morning of the delivery of that first load, I found John, the driver, parked up in the yard, having driven the wrong way down the one-way system. He shook my hand and said, "Mr Wyatt, I have five tonnes overweight but, because I don't speak English, they waved me through."

The buildings were quickly erected, and we set about increasing pig numbers, buying breeding females and boars from the Northern Pig Development Company at Beverley in Yorkshire. When we were in full production, my accountant, Keith Keyte, said to me, "Why do you bother with any other sort of farming when pigs are making as much money as this?" But I was reminded of what Donald Crichton-Miller had written to me after he came to visit: "You are doing reasonably well and it is important that you do not have all your eggs in one basket." How right he would be proved.

Hillacre Farm, running down to the lake

Our new fattening house was the first in the country to have a slatted floor and naturally attracted a lot of interest from within the industry. Not long after we started using it I took a call from Stephen Curtis, whose father John had started the very successful Northern Pig Development Company, asking if he could pay us a visit. It soon appeared that it would be, quite literally, a flying visit, as he asked me where the nearest airfield was. We decided it must be Dunkeswell, high up in the Blackdown Hills, so I set off to meet him there at 11 o'clock. By the time I got there he was waiting for me, so I drove him back to Hillacre, gave him a lightning tour of the pig unit, drove him back to Hemyock for a pub lunch at the Catherine Wheel and by early afternoon he was disappearing over the horizon again in his twin-engined plane, for his 200-mile flight home.

Interesting people, the Curtis family. John owned racehorses as well as pigs. He once gave me a tip that one of his horses would win a big hurdle race at Haydock Park and that I could safely bet my shirt on it. His wife told me not to be stupid, so I didn't. Needless to say, it won.

I have always believed that there is no better investment than land, so when, in 1982, I received a telephone call from Brigadier 'Tuppy' Forbes to say that he was selling 20 acres of land at Burrow Hill, adjoining Brewers, and would I like to make a sealed bid for it, I jumped at the chance. After checking with Chris, who was equally keen, I went to see him to suggest that, rather than selling the land, he should join Fitzhead Farms as a partner. This was not well received. "I don't want you for a partner," was his blunt response.

So I decided to be equally blunt, telling the Brigadier that I wasn't going to put in a sealed bid but that we would give him £20,000 for the land. He was happy with that, unlike several other prospective purchasers who'd been planning to put in their sealed bids, now pre-empted!

After we'd settled the deal he asked me if I could recommend an accountant who could advise him on what to do with the money, so I suggested my own accountant, Keith Keyte. He did indeed have some good advice: buy some land with it!

By the time Fitzhead Farms was fully up and running, there was no shortage of interest in what we were doing with the merger of our two businesses. So, despite Chris' misgivings, we entered the Somerset Centre for Farm Management Farms Competition in 1985 and 1986, winning the large farm category in both years. As a result of that, I was asked the following year to judge the Nottinghamshire farms competition, taking with me Terry Miller from Stogursey to fill the gap in my knowledge when it came to dairy farming. We had great fun judging, both then and later in Hampshire, learned a lot and both made and met good friends, among them Jean and Neil Farley at West Twisted and Jack Edney, who was on the Hampshire committee and with whom I'd been at school.

The arable side of the farm was not neglected. In 1984 Robert harvested 50 tonnes of wheat from one ten-acre field – five tonnes per acre, at 14% moisture, delivered to Devon Grain. I told father about what was, by any standards, a remarkable achievement. "How many sacks (2 cwt each) is that?" he asked. "Fifty," I replied. "That's not possible," he said. I asked him if he'd seen Neil Armstrong walk on the moon. "Yes," he said, "I saw it and I believe it. But I'll never believe it is possible to grow 50 sacks of wheat per acre." And he went to his grave not long afterwards, still not believing it.

Fitzhead Farms was a success by almost any yardstick. We'd made money, we'd worked well together, we'd saved costs and we'd won both farm competitions and environmental awards. But Chris was insistent that we should take our two star-herdsmen, John Smith and John Thompson, into the partnership and this did not go down well with the younger generation – Chris's son Roger and my son Robert. Roger had been running his own travel company in Africa but had decided that he wanted to come home to farm. How were we going to fit him in? Nor was Robert a natural co-operator. "We're just subsidising the Shaplands," he would insist to me, and tensions grew.

One morning in 1989 Chris rang me to say that he was having a meeting with Roger and Robert and that I wasn't invited. "Why not?" I asked. "Because you'll have too much to say," I was told.

By midday they had decided to split the partnership. Thankfully it was all fairly straightforward because the valuations had all been agreed in advance. Because of the pig unit at Hillacre, I ended up paying out a lot. I still think it was the wrong thing to do. It pays to know when you're well off, and in Fitzhead Farms we were well off.

But there was nothing to be done, so Robert and I set about running the business ourselves. This didn't last long. Robert was hunting three days a week and shooting on a fourth, expecting to do his bit on Sundays and other odd days while Reggie Westcott and I carried the workload. In the end Robert and I decided that our partnership just wasn't working and we parted company. Robert went into property development and barn conversions and made an outstanding success of it. I suppose it just goes to show that some are born co-operators and some prefer to go it alone.

The pig unit came to a sad end as well. Our accountant Keith Keyte had set up an arrangement whereby John Thompson would buy me out of it in instalments over a period of years. But then the herd was struck down with Blue Ear disease, possibly picked up, so our vets suggested, from the pigs in the lorries which passed close to the unit on their way to the abattoir at Wiveliscombe.

Poor John lost everything, and I was hit hard as well; what I had earmarked for my pension fund gone up in smoke. Fortunately, I was able to pay all of the creditors in full, which was more than a lot of them had expected.

Fitzhead Farms wasn't the only farming partnership to break up at around this time. Mary and I had been growing apart for some time, and I had become increasingly close to Olive Parsons, whom I had first met, many years previously, at a Young Conservatives meeting. So I made up my mind to leave. That was on 14 February 1986. In the course of the day I attended two funerals and in the evening led a members' revolt at Burnham and Berrow Golf Club at a tense and highly charged Special General Meeting, before driving back to Wellington to move in with Olive. It was quite a day!

I should say that Mary was in no way to blame for the split up. I just felt it would be for the best for both of us if I moved on. Needless to say, my decision provoked any amount of gossip, comment and advice. At the golf club, my good friend Denis Clyde-Smith made no bones about it: "Your place is at Hillacre, old man," he told me. But I had considered all the pros and cons and reached the firm conclusion that there would be less upheaval if I moved out. Jayne and Robert were adults and would cope, and the farm was running so smoothly that I didn't need to be living on site. It is a decision that, for all the upset at the time and the financial consequences, bearing in mind that Mary's family had a substantial stake in the business, I have never for one moment regretted.

Considering the complications of the divorce settlement, matters were concluded remarkably amicably, thanks not least to the constructive attitude taken by Mary's solicitor, Nicholas Arrow, even if we did have some fairly robust discussions! Given that it had been Mary's father's money which had financed the purchase of Brewers, that went to the Trustees appointed to look after her, Robert and Jayne. I kept Hillacre. In an ideal world it might have been better the other way round, but the tax implications ruled that out.

Having lived with Olive at Westford just outside Wellington from 1986, we decided that it would be good to move back to somewhere near the farm. After considering the options, Robert, on behalf of the family trustees, agreed that we could develop the barns at Brewers Farm, where I had kept cattle and pigs back in the 1960s. This proved to be anything but straightforward. First, Trevor Abell on his JCB had the greatest difficulty digging out the concrete pens. Then I had a terrible run-in with a planning officer for Taunton Deane Borough Council (where Olive still worked, as PA to the Chief Executive) over his insistence that we should have a metal pipe for a chimney rather than a proper stone-built job. It ended with me ordering him off the farm and telling him never to set foot on it again! That was eventually sorted out with the planner's boss and work started on 2 January 1992. By May that year, enough had been done to enable us to move in and by August all was complete. That was another decision I have never regretted!

The barns at Brewers Farm – 1992 and now

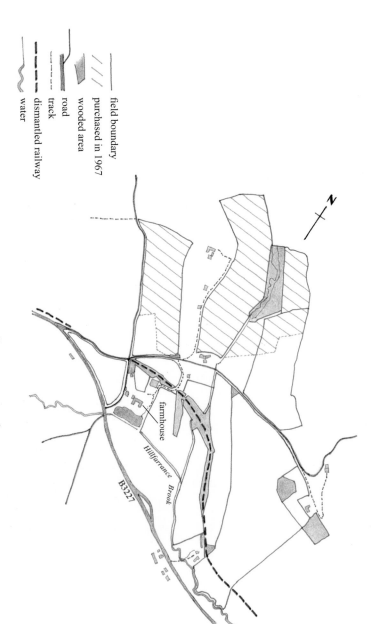

Hillacre Farm today

field boundary
purchased in 1967
wooded area
road
track
dismantled railway
water

N

B3227

farmhouse

Hillfarrance Brook

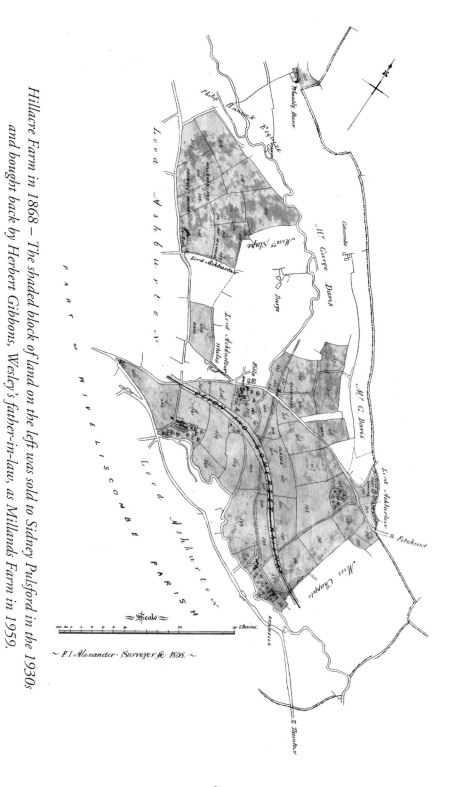

Hillacre Farm in 1868 – The shaded block of land on the left was sold to Sidney Pulsford in the 1930s and bought back by Herbert Gibbons, Wesley's father-in-law, as Millands Farm in 1959.

7

Community service

The Wyatts and Reeds had always done their bit for the local community. Father was a long-standing member of both the Wiveliscombe Without Parish Council and Wellington Rural District Council, retiring when he reached the age of 70 in 1967. Soon afterwards, I had a call from Sydney Pulsford, a Wiveliscombe Without councillor as well as being Chairman of Somerset County Council, to ask me to attend a Parish Council meeting. In those days parish councillors were appointed rather than elected whenever there were vacancies, which I gathered was what Sydney had in mind for me. So I turned up, together with two other local farmers, Tony Hill and Philip Hawkins, who, it appeared, were also in line for appointment. It was explained to us that we would become councillors after we had attended a few meetings to gain some experience, which was what happened.

The Chairman of the Council was Dick Hawkins, a Wilscombe butcher, and his two right-hand men were Sydney Pulsford and Herbert Dascombe. Whenever a decision was needed, Dick would ask each of these two in turn what they thought and, if they indicated agreement, he would announce: "Well, that's passed." None of this was particularly democratic but it seemed to work. It was only when we were amalgamated with Wiveliscombe Within to form a single council that elections were held. I was duly elected and remained a conscientious member of the council until 1985, when I failed to be re-elected because of my recent divorce. Such too is local democracy.

When it comes to party politics, I have always taken a lively interest without being particularly partisan. Coming from a nonconformist family, I would have been expected to be a Liberal or Labour supporter, as I'm sure was the case with Grandfather Reed. But the Tories were traditionally the party for the landed interest, and that proved to be the decisive factor when it came to my politics, despite the fact that the

1947 Agriculture Act, which brought stability and relative prosperity to farming through the 50s and 60s, had been the work of a Labour government. When I first joined the Young Farmers in the late 1940s, Taunton's MP was Victor Collins, the only Labour MP the constituency has ever elected, and despite the fact that his family business was willow growing and basket-making – a cause very close to Somerset hearts – he became a bit of a target to us enthusiastic farming youngsters in Wiveliscombe YFC. We would travel around to his meetings, frequently getting ourselves thrown out for asking awkward questions.

However, our activities must have made some sort of mark, not so much in the fact that Mr Collins lost his seat at the 1950 General Election, as in the call I received from the Conservatives a few years later after Edward du Cann had become the member, asking me if I would like to be chairman of the Taunton constituency Young Conservatives. I accepted and did my fair share of meetings and canvassing. On one occasion when we were out canvassing together, I listened to Edward du Cann talking to a group of ladies, saying things that I knew perfectly well were stretching the bounds of veracity to their absolute limits. As we moved on, I asked him how he felt about saying things that he must have known were untrue. "It's all just part of the job, my dear," was his reply, "just part of the job." And I'm sorry to have to conclude that it still is, judging by much more recent political shenanigans.

But by and large, those were settled, stable years for politics and for agriculture. We enjoyed a framework of policies and support which enabled an enthusiastic, hard-working and determined young farmer like myself to get on in the world. Harold Macmillan may well have had a point when he said in 1957 that "most of our people have never had it so good".

These days I am more of an old-fashioned Whig than a Tory, who believes that government should come from the centre ground, rather than from one extreme or the other. I sometimes despair at world events, whether it be the dreadful polarisation of American politics or the vicious nationalism of that man Putin and his brutal invasion of Ukraine. I wish I had more faith that he will get his comeuppance, preferably in this world rather than the next.

At the organ

But whilst I may have often thought globally and still do, I have always done my best to act locally, and not just through the local council. Hence taking on the chairmanship of the War Memorial Recreation Ground Committee and of the Cricket Club and in 1976, at a parish council meeting, I proposed that consideration should be given to forming a local history society, as I had always been interested in the history and heritage of my town. So a small group was formed, which met in Dick Hawkins' bungalow. Among its members were Bernadette Rowe, Dixon Luxton, Clare Baker and Stanley Batey, plus myself. From that emerged the Wiveliscombe Historical Society, Chairman RW Wyatt.

Our meetings were always well attended and created much interest in the town as we unearthed all sorts of information about the parish and parish folk. Our leading light was undoubtedly Stanley Batey, a retired teacher and archivist, and when he sadly died a lot of the steam went out of the venture; eventually the Historical Society was merged with the Civic Society. Even so, I like to think that we played our part in awakening interest in Wiveliscombe's history, an interest which would lead in time to Susan Farrington's remarkable book 'Wiveliscombe: A History', to which many of our founders contributed.

Chapel and, later, church have always been a big part of my life. I think my mother would like me to have become a Methodist minister, but that was something on which we had to agree to differ. But she did succeed in binding me into the nonconformist community by arranging for me to learn to play first the piano and later the organ, no doubt planning all along that I would end up playing the organ in Wiveliscombe Methodist Chapel.

I started piano lessons in Milverton at the age of six or seven, and by the time I went to Taunton School I was already being taught to play the organ by Herbert Knott at St Mary's in Taunton. The great organ at Taunton School was a wonderful instrument, and by the time I left school I was, if not exactly the finished article, then certainly more than capable of playing the role that mother had always had in mind for me. For 37 years I played the organ for the Chapel and thoroughly enjoyed it, even if did prevent me playing golf on a Sunday after I had taken up the game.

By the mid 1980s, I was Secretary and Treasurer of the Chapel, besides being the organist, but I was playing for an ageing and diminishing flock, and the money to keep us going was running out. So I called the regulars together and put it to them that our average age was about 80, pointing out that "there's another lot just across the road, worshipping the same God, so why don't we go over there and join them?"

So they agreed to invite the Anglican vicar, Chris Marshall, to come to a meeting and he did enough to persuade them to give the Church of England a try. On the way out I congratulated Chris on his diplomacy and added the thought that all we needed to do now to make the arrangement a success was to compromise.

"Over my dead body," was his reply.

Sure enough, the Methodists gradually drifted away to the Chapel in Milverton and, after two years or so, Olive and I were the only ones left. In the meantime I had been appointed to the Parochial Church Council and had become great friends with Chris. He cut a fine figure, riding around the parish on his horse, lifting his hat to every parishioner he encountered, even if actually visiting his flock was not his greatest strength. At just about every PCC meeting he would pass me a note saying "Pub afterwards?" And so it came to pass.

One slightly unusual contribution that I made to the local community was to burn down a church. The circumstances were as follows. Towards the end of the nineteenth century, the inhabitants of Croford decided that they would like to worship rather more locally, instead of having to trail into Wiveliscombe once, or even twice, every Sunday. My grandfather, Robert James Wyatt, made available one of his barns at Hillacre for services. But this was clearly less than satisfactory, and so a fund-raising campaign was launched to raise the money to build a church, which would effectively be a chapel of Wiveliscombe Parish Church. The money was duly raised – grandfather playing a prominent role – and the Church of the Holy Trinity was built. It was a modest structure, of wood and tin, and it was sited down by the Hillfarrance Brook – rather too near to the brook, as it turned out.

Whilst popular at first, attendance gradually dwindled until by the 1950s it had effectively been abandoned; a rusting, crumbling, unsightly glorified shed, slipping slowly into the brook. When Chris Marshall was appointed vicar of the parent church, the churchwarden, Dixon Luxton, decided that something needed to be done about the Croford ruin, so that Chris wouldn't have to worry about it when he took up his post. So, as a man who believed in action rather than words, he approached me and asked me if I would burn it down for him, no doubt calculating that, as a nonconformist, I wouldn't have any religious qualms!

So I stuffed the church full of straw and set light to it, and it went up like a giant firework, setting fire to the nearest telegraph pole as it blazed. The fire brigade were soon on the scene. I advised them to concentrate their efforts on the telegraph pole, but to let the church and various bits of other rubbish, which had been abandoned by a man called Gassy Harris in the field next to it, to burn. "But we're here to put the fire out!" expostulated the head fireman. It was too late. The church was burned to the ground, and now not a trace of it remains. I suppose it was technically arson, but nobody seemed to mind.

Church of the Holy Trinity in flames

Retiring from full-time farming in 2006 meant that I had more time on my hands, so I volunteered to act as a driver for Wivey Link, a subsidised community transport service. Most of the time I drove a Yaris and took some of the town's more senior citizens shopping or to hospital or sometimes just to visit friends. I particularly remember two occasions, on both of which I blotted my copybook.

The first was when I was driving Wivey Link's larger vehicle, capable of carrying wheelchairs. My passenger on this occasion was Robert Walton, who had once worked for the potato company, and as I wheeled him into the vehicle we both agreed that the standard practice of strapping wheelchair and occupant in was daft, because if there was an accident, it would be that much more difficult to get him out. So I said, "Hold on Robert" and drove up from Northgate into the Square. But someone must have seen what was going on, for I was reported to the office and given a mild reprimand. I never drove that vehicle again.

The other incident occurred when I collected Christopher Lindsay from Fitzhead to take him to a drawing class in Wiveliscombe. He was a lovely man, a former army officer, who had suffered a serious stroke which had left him disabled and difficult to converse with. He had his own vocabulary, with words beginning with either an f or a p the most used.

"Fantastic," he said when I picked him up. As we arrived in Wiveliscombe he said "pub in S"(quare). I said I would take him to the Bear after his class and collect him before one o'clock.

"Fantastic," he said again. I duly dropped him off and collected him. We'd barely gone a quarter of a mile before he came out with "Piss", prompting me to drive quickly out of town and stop by the roadside so that he could relieve himself. But again someone must have spotted us, as I was given another reprimand for taking Christopher to the pub. Such are the rewards which Good Samaritans sometimes receive! Undeterred, I carried on driving for Wivey Link and very much enjoying it, until I was 80 and they told me I could no longer be insured.

8

Liscombe and other run-ins with government

Liscombe, high up on Exmoor to the north of Dulverton, was one of a string of 'Experimental Husbandry Farms' set up by the Ministry of Agriculture in the 1950s to develop and test new and possibly better ways of growing crops and rearing livestock, so as to boost productivity and, in the process, leave farmers better off. The EHFs were a vital under-pinning of the Government's farm advisory service, NAAS and later ADAS, and did much good work. Each farm had an Advisory Committee made up of prominent local farmers drawn from the areas they served. I was invited to join the Liscombe Committee in the late 1970s, presumably on the strength of our highly successful sheep enterprise, and by 1988 I'd been elected to chair it.

It was at that point that Mrs Thatcher stepped in. Committed as she was to reducing the size of Government – a worthy cause if ever there was one – she cast a beady eye over the EHFs and didn't much like what she saw. Here was the Government carrying out research which, in many cases, would directly benefit the businesses which made use of it. Surely this was a case where the beneficiaries, rather than the taxpayer, should be footing the bill?

So a report was commissioned – the Barnes Report – which did indeed conclude that the so-called 'near market' research engaged in by the EHFs should be funded by farmers and that the first EHF to which this principle would be applied was Liscombe, with the explicit threat that if the farmers failed to stump up their share of the funding, the farm would close. Why Liscombe? Because its Open Days regularly attracted over 5,000 farmers and its work, particularly on silage additives (which it demonstrated were largely a waste of money), was highly valued by the livestock farming community across the South-West. The fact that Liscombe was championed by the region's most successful and highest profile agricultural co-operative, Mole Valley Farmers, helped

Liscombe Research

* practical and commercial *
* run by farmers for farmers *
* based on the best scientific practice *
* carried out by skilled and experienced staff *

The _Best_ Research for the Best Grassland Farmers!

as well. If farmers anywhere could be persuaded to rally round and help fund their local EHF, then surely it would be in the South-West with Liscombe.

The announcement was made in March 1988, and after some initial scepticism as to whether anything could be done, other than to lobby fruitlessly for a change of policy, a rather more positive approach emerged. The NFU became involved, as did Mole Valley. At a meeting in Exeter I suggested that the easiest way to raise the money would be through a supplement on NFU subscriptions. This was greeted with silence! Nonetheless, agreement was reached (a) that we should attempt to negotiate the best possible terms from MAFF and (b) that if a reasonable deal on costs could be achieved, farmers should be invited to pay a flat rate £50/year each towards whatever the cost might be.

So the NFU's Anthony Gibson, MVF's hard-bitten Managing Director John James and I set off for London to negotiate a deal with MAFF. This was only a limited success. The new company that we proposed to form would have to pay MAFF a total of £400,000 – the best part of a million pounds at present-day values – in return for running the farm and continuing with most of its research programme over the first three years. Beyond that, a grossly inflated 'full economic cost' would have to be covered. If that was discouraging, the response from the farming community was anything but. A 'Save Liscombe' campaign succeeded in persuading nearly 1500 farmers to sign standing orders committing them to pay £50 a year for three years, as well as raising tens of thousands of pounds in sponsorship. By the end of June I was in a position to write to the minister responsible, the magnificent Baroness Jean Trumpington, to say that we were in a position to go ahead. 'Liscombe Research', as the new venture was called, was born.

Malcolm Appleton, who had not long succeeded Len Gurnett as the farm's director, worked out a more than worthwhile programme of research and we were fortunate in having a first-class committee, Board as it became, with Anthony Gibson and his highly efficient PA Helen Robinson as our secretariat. It is worth listing the Board in full, considering how much hard work they put in, all at their own expense: Geoff Hewett, Trull; David Cray, Camelford; Brian Peace, Rackenford; John Kingman, Dartmoor Prison Farm; David Moore, Torrington; Eric Norman, Brendon Hills; Hector Delbridge, North Molton; Robin Slade, Exton; John James, Mole Valley Farmers.

Committee meetings could be lively affairs, with any number of different opinions being expressed. At the end of the debate I would ask Anthony Gibson to summarise our disparate views in a resolution, which he would do with such diplomacy and skill that it would invariably be passed unanimously! It's helpful, if you're a chairman, to have a man of words alongside.

*Baroness
Trumpington*

Our official launch was delayed until November, on a dismal day when the fog lay thick across the slopes of Winsford Hill. Baroness Trumpington had to cut the State Opening of Parliament to be there, along with John McCleod, MAFF's Director of Experimental Farms. The pair of them arrived at the farm by car from Taunton Station. She got out of the car with a pile of papers and said to me, "Wesley, I know bugger all about this!" But she proved to be a quick learner. Introductions concluded, I took her into a side room to meet the staff, a room which had 'no smoking' signs on every wall. These, the Parliamentary Secretary (Lords) for Agriculture, Fisheries and Food appeared conveniently to be blind to. "Is there an ashtray somewhere?" she boomed, and one such was rapidly provided. But when it came to the opening ceremonies, she was magnificent, resplendent in scarlet, striking just the right note. It was an uplifting day, full of hope.

At its conclusion I presented the Baroness with a bottle of George IV whisky, which I'd been told was her favourite tipple. Some weeks later, when I bumped into John McCleod, he told me that by the time they reached Paddington that evening the bottle was empty! A great lady.

I carried on as Chairman for another year or so before handing over to Geoff Hewett, a top-class farmer and a good man, and much good work was done during our three years in charge. But the Liscombe story does not have a happy ending. At the end of those first three years, MAFF's financial demands proved insupportable at a time when West County livestock farmers were making little or no money, and Liscombe Research quietly folded.

Still, I enjoyed my involvement with Liscombe, which gave me the chance to meet all sorts of interesting and distinguished farming people, none more so than Ossie Johnson, who was Vice-Chairman of the Redesdale EHF in Northumberland. Ossie was a renowned gardener with one of the highest gardens in England. He and his family were pillars of the local chapel, each playing a different instrument to provide music for the services. They didn't drink, of course, and there wasn't even a television in the farmhouse. Ossie produced breeding sheep from Scotch Blackface ewes put to Bluefaced Leicester rams, and very fine sheep they were too.

Being Chairman of the Liscombe Advisory Committee was not my only role with MAFF. Several years before our 'privatisation', at an EHF chairmen's meeting in London, I was approached by the then minister, John Gummer. "I've heard a lot about you and it is not good," was his rather disconcerting opening gambit. But he went on to ask me if I would be prepared to join his 'Ruminants Group', one of several groups which had been put together to advise on how government-funded research work was being managed. This proved to be both a painful and a largely fruitless undertaking. Our meetings were held either in a subterranean room in Whitehall or up in Edinburgh. On one occasion, when I was suffering from a broken ankle, the return flight from Edinburgh was diverted from Bristol to Exeter, which involved a long and painful bus journey to retrieve my car. I wouldn't have minded but for the fact that when our report was published, including some criticism of the Civil Service, it was promptly swept under the carpet and a new group formed.

This merely served to reinforce the impression I had gained during my earlier years on the Liscombe Committee. Our meetings often involved a farm visit – including one to Fitzhead Farms, where we provided a splendid 'Taste of Somerset' lunch – followed by a dinner at the Caernarvon Arms at Brushford and then the committee meeting proper the following day at Liscombe. We wouldn't get the minutes of the meeting until the agenda for our next meeting was sent out, the best part of six months later, and they never, but never, seemed to correspond with the notes that I had taken.

Exasperated by this, I decided to go right to the top and telephoned Sir Michael Franklin, MAFF's Permanent Secretary and fellow Old Tauntonian. He agreed to a meeting and I took him out to lunch at the Commonwealth Club. We had a fine time reminiscing about school but, when it came to the substance of my complaint, all he had to offer was: "That is your opinion." What a lot of effort to go through just to demonstrate what I'd felt all along, that the Civil Service merely soaks up criticism like blotting paper.

9

Old Tauntonians

I joined the Taunton School Old Boys Association, as it was known then, almost as soon as I left school, and the Old Tauntonians, as they eventually became, have been an important part of my life ever since, the cradle of any number of lasting friendships.

My first engagement with them came not long after I'd joined, when I was rung up by John Dearden, a housemaster at the school, asking me if I could pick him up and drive him to a skittles match at Lower Weare, not far from Wedmore, where the Western branch of the Association had a match against the Bristol branch. It wasn't only skittles that us old boys played. There was rugby, an annual cricket match against the school and, rather later in my case, Old Tauntonian golf, to which I took like a duck to water.

As a keen and regular participant in all of these activities, I soon found myself being given positions to fill. In time I became Chairman of the Western branch, President of the Association (as it still then was) and President of the Old Tauntonians Golf Society. In my year as President, the golf team qualified to play in the Halford Hewitt tournament, which is contested at Deal and Royal St George's Golf Clubs by teams of public school old boys from across the country. In my year Taunton played Wellington College in the first round at Royal St George's, a tough draw, and we duly got beaten. My main contribution to the proceedings was to go into the locker room after the match and – tongue in cheek – berate my side for taking four hours to play a round of foursomes. Another happy memory of that day is that my opposite number for Wellington was James Pease-Watkin, who had played in the Stocks foursomes at Burnham.

What had paved the way for my eventual elevation to Old Tauntonian President was a phone call I took in 1971 from Eric Wright, a Taunton master whom I knew from the golf course. Did I know, he asked,

Three generations of Old Tauntonians
Tom, Robert and me

that Barclays Bank were running a competition in which schools and other organisations could compete to put together a business plan for an imaginary farm, with decisions to be made every month? The idea appealed, and we decided to have a go, the only school to do so. We put together a combined team of pupils and parents and engaged Stan Farrer, a local farming consultant, to put our plans together. I'm glad to be able to say that we made it to the final, at the National Agricultural Centre at Stoneleigh, alongside four other teams. The task of presenting our plans fell to me, and we finished as runners-up to a team from Northern Ireland, whose plans seemed to me to be complete pie in the sky! Norman Roberts, the headmaster, made the trip to see how we got on and was sufficiently impressed to put me down as a future OT President.

This came about eventually in 1980. Edward du Cann spoke at my inaugural dinner in London, where my own beef was served at table by Ivor Reed, Desmond Baker, David Hobbs and Bryan Brighton. I thoroughly enjoyed my year, visiting Old Tauntonian branches the length and breadth of the country, for the OTs are reputed to have the biggest membership of any old boys' (and girls'!) association. Olive and I have remained very much involved in the school, the OTs and, most rewardingly, the Foundation which provides scholarships for deserving youngsters whose parents can't afford the school fees, ever since.

My other noteworthy service to my old school was triggered by an encounter with Crikey at an Old Tauntonians Whitsun week-end. He asked me to take on the running of something called the 'Gerrard Fund', named in honour of Ron Gerrard, an Old Tauntonian England rugby international, whose biography – 'Men of a Stout Countenance' – Crikey had written. That and the fact that his widow Molly was a legendary President of Bath Rugby was really all I knew, but of course I said yes. Crikey's wish was my command! It turned out that the fund had been created to endow a scholarship to help a school leaver who had achieved some sporting distinction at school with funding their further education, and it was in a poor state of health. It seemed to me that the only beneficiaries were the

Crikey holding forth

trustees themselves, who enjoyed a good lunch in Bath every year, paid for out of the fund. My suggestion that they ditch the lunch and use the money for its intended purpose was not well received, but I carried on anyway. The lunch was scrapped, the money was invested profitably, and Olive and I invited Duncan Gerrard, Ron and Molly's son, to lunch and a discussion about the fund's future. To cut a long story short, this resulted in Duncan (who had actually been to school at Cheltenham College) being made an honorary Old Tauntonian. When he died, he left his money partly to the church where he worshipped in Dartmouth and partly to the Gerrard Fund, which has never looked back.

Old Tauntonians may be found in virtually every corner of the globe, and perhaps particularly in Capetown, to which a number of OTs had moved from Zimbabwe, when Robert Mugabe took over from Ian Smith in 1980. So when Olive and I made one of our trips to South Africa, I decided to contact Bill Shepherd-Wilson who was a surgeon in Groote Schuur Hospital to see if we could arrange a meeting of OTs.

In the event it wasn't so much a meeting as a party, given by Bill and his wife Wendy. It turned out to be a memorable occasion, thanks not least to the company of Pam and Fred Dawe, retired tobacco growers, with Fred turning out to be one of the most enthusiastic OTs I've ever met!

Fred Dawe

Old Tauntonians in Bruges
Jane and David Hobbs (back) with Olive and me

It was on that trip that Olive and I, conscious of the ubiquity of OTs, were discussing how long we might be in South Africa before someone we knew turned up. Sure enough, as we were walking out of the dining room, I spotted someone who looked remarkably like Gordon Jackman, Secretary of the OT Golf Society, who had arrived at Taunton School at the same time as me and had been in the next dormitory. Several meals together and much reminiscing ensued.

Later when I told Crikey that we had been entertained by Bill Shepherd-Wilson, he said, "Ah, Wes, difficult father. What man would send his son to school in England in wartime from the safety of Rhodesia? It must have been Fred Dawe's influence, his love for the school, which brought it about." Some years later when Fred had lost his wife, he spent his 80th birthday with us at Tommy Brewers.

None of the many friendships I have made through the Old Tauntonians has meant more to me than that with Bryan Brighton. It was cricket that brought us together, when we both turned out for the OTs not long after I'd left school. I had known Bryan at school

Bryan and Marion Brighton and their four daughters

but hadn't much liked him, because he was a prefect and his preferred punishment for any of my misdemeanours was to make me clean the filthy old gas ring on which the prefects made toast. By the time I met him again on the cricket field he was at Nottingham University, studying agriculture and playing rugby in the centre for Coventry, who were then one of the best teams in the country. We found much to talk about and became great friends.

His ambition was to become a farmer, preferably in Devon, but he rang me some time afterwards to say that Devon farms were too expensive and that instead he had bought a 'twitchy' farm in Lincolnshire – that is to say, a farm infested with couch grass, one of the farmer's greatest enemies. He financed the purchase by finding someone in London to lend him the money and then lease it back to him at a market rent, the capital being repaid as and when he could afford it. In those days this was a pioneering arrangement.

The farm was Middle Fen Farm, Washingborough. The main enterprise was dairy cows, which were milked by his wife Marion while Bryan travelled the country playing rugby for Moseley and Coventry. I asked him how he could afford so much time away from the farm. "The boot money just about covers it," he replied.

By the time I first went to see him in Lincolnshire, the family – Bryan, Marion and their four lovely daughters – Sandra, Susan and the twins Jacqui and Gina – had moved a mile or so up the road to Poplar Bank Farm. This was every bit as difficult as Middle Fen, on peaty soil from which bog oaks had regularly to be excavated and in which machinery regularly got stuck. He employed two men, one of them a fireman, who only worked when he was off duty, and the other whom he fetched from the local prison.

I followed Bryan's progress with interest, and we travelled often together to Scotland, on one occasion staying with Betty and Sandy Simpson, from whom Deane Growers bought seed potatoes, and to the Royal Show, for which we stayed with Bryan's brother David. He was another Old Tauntonian, who went to work first as a salesman, then as a manager for Silcock's, the animal feed merchants. He ended up going into business on his own account, devising something which he called the 'Dover Plan', a get-rich-quick scheme devised by Tiny Rowland, which he would eventually sell a million pounds worth of, for which he won a very expensive watch. "You must buy it, you can't lose," he insisted to me over the phone. No sooner had I put the phone down than I had a call from Bryan. "On no account have anything to do with the Dover Plan," he advised. So I didn't.

Our friendship had a sad ending. In October 1982 I had a call from his daughter Susan to say that Bryan was not at all well and that I ought to come and see him before it was too late. He had developed lung cancer, almost certainly caused by all the fen dust he had inhaled in those days before tractor cabs. So I went straightaway and we spent a memorable day together, talking about the times we had spent together and the joys and sorrows of our farming lives. Some days later, he phoned. Clearly fighting for breath, he said "This is it, chum," and he died that night.

Other good friends from the OTs were Paul and Mary Hunning (rather better known as Mary Berry, the cookery writer and broadcaster), Barry and Anne White, Tony and Evy Guest and Jane Legg (formerly Hobbs). For many years we held an annual reunion, involving a weekend away somewhere and much reminiscing about the old days. Sadly, but I suppose inevitably, we are now down to just the Hunnings and ourselves.

One of the best things about my involvement with the Old Tauntonians was the opportunities it gave me to meet and talk with Crichton-Miller who, from the fearsome headmaster of 1943, was to become something of a mentor and exemplar. On one occasion he and I were with a group of Old Tauntonians at the Hunnings' house in Buckinghamshire, celebrating their sixtieth birthdays. We were discussing a Taunton housemaster called AG Marshall, known to his pupils as Bingie, with whom I had fallen out over my choice of Wills East as my senior house in 1946, as opposed to Fairwater, which was Bingie's house.

"Ah, Wes," said Crichton-Miller. "What you have to remember is that Bingie suffered from an inferiority complex in comparison with his brother LP Marshall, who was better than him at virtually everything. He had major hang-ups."

Crikey was an imposing figure but he didn't always get his way. When I relinquished the OT Presidency in 1980, a service was held in the school chapel, taken by my Prebend at Wiveliscombe, the Rev Chris Marshall. He impressed everyone, Crikey included, so much so that he told me he wanted to carry him off to Compton in Berkshire, where he, Crikey, was Churchwarden. I was having nothing of it!

One other very important contribution which Taunton School has made to Olive and my lives was to provide the setting for our wedding celebrations. This was on 22 April 1989, with a service in the school chapel. It was quite an occasion, perhaps the highlights being 'An air with variations on Holsworthy church bells' by Samuel Wesley, which I had first heard played on the school organ by George Thalben Ball, and the school choir sang Hubert Parry's anthem 'I was glad'. I am not usually an emotional sort, but my eyes filled with tears of joy at that.

Wedding Day, April 1989
Ruth Senior, Fred Griffin, Olive, Me, Mary Summers, Gordon Senior

10

This sporting life

I owe my interest in sport to my father, who was a passionate supporter of Wiveliscombe Rugby Football Club and Somerset County Cricket Club. Not long after I left Taunton School, he took me to watch Somerset play the 1948 Australian tourists at the County Ground. Even without Bradman the Australians racked up 560/5 on the first day and went on to win by the little matter of an innings and 374 runs! But what I remember most vividly of that day was a century by the 18 year-old left-hander Neil Harvey. It was, quite simply, the greatest innings I have seen. Some of the innings I saw the great Harold Gimblett play weren't far behind, and another favourite was Micky Walford, a hockey international and master at Sherborne School, who could only turn out for Somerset during the summer holidays.

I had enjoyed my cricket and rugby at school so when I left I joined Wiveliscombe Rugby Club and Fitzhead Cricket Club. But after my first year back home, father said I would have to choose one or the other, as he was fed up with being left to do all the farm work on Saturdays all the year round. So I chose cricket and joined Wiveliscombe Cricket Club in 1953, for which I played for the next 17 years as an all-rounder. I wasn't one of the club's star players by any means, although I can't have been that bad, as I was invited to play for both RJO Meyer's XI ('Boss' Meyer being the Millfield founder and headmaster and a former captain of Somerset) and the Somerset Stragglers, which had been founded many years before as a sort of amateur adjunct to the county side.

It was the cricket that introduced me to golf. In 1970 I captained a midweek XI on a trip to Gloucester. The team included a couple of visitors, old Shebbearians from the school in North Devon. It was one of this pair who hauled me out of bed at five o'clock on our second morning – barely an hour after I had turned in – to tell me that he and some of the others were going to play golf, taking me as a caddy. The course he had chosen was Stinchcombe Hill, high above Dursley and the Severn Vale. When we reached the 17th tee – the line from which is marked by the monument to the great William Tyndale, who gave us the first translation of the Bible into English and was executed for his pains – I had a five-iron thrust into my hands and told to have a go. The shot wasn't a bad one, and I remember saying at the time that this golfing lark was a great deal better than chasing a cricket ball around the boundary for half a day.

If you are taking up golf, then go and get some lessons from a pro, was the advice I received, and very sound it was too. So I went to see Ken Fear at Taunton and Pickeridge, who took me into a shed and watched me hit a few balls. "You can certainly hit the ball, sir," he commented, "but slow down." It was good advice, which I have tried to follow ever since, not always with success!

The first hole that I played was the first at Taunton and Pickeridge, in the company of Ken Fear. It was a par four which I played in four. "Does that mean I'm a scratch golfer?" I said to Ken in my triumph. "No, sir," he replied.

I joined the club soon afterwards and fell in with a group of members who played golf on the championship links of Burnham and Berrow on the north Somerset coast every Thursday. The first time I walked into the clubhouse I was so impressed that I said to my companions that this was a club of which I'd really love to be a member. Our conversation was overheard by a man who would become a great friend, Squadron Leader Denis Clyde-Smith DSO DFC, war hero, no sufferer of fools and a thoroughly good egg. "Come with me, old man," said Denis, leading me into the office of the Secretary, Clifford Burden, who was instructed to "sign him up, old man." Which he did, so that there and then I became a member of Burnham and Berrow GC, an institution which has brought me more pleasure than I can find words to describe.

Driving from Croford to Burnham in the days before the M5 was built through Somerset was quite a trek, taking in Taunton, North Petherton, Bridgwater and Highbridge en route. My early visits were

Golf in the snow at Burnham and Berrow

often in the company of Frank Mead, a Taunton car salesman who had recently bought the White Hart in Wiveliscombe, to play in the Friday Club. Burnham and Berrow Golf Club was a fun place to be in 1970, and Frank was a fun man to share it with. Besides the golf, we played snooker and billiards and would often be joined by Oliver Down from Bristol, as well as more local members.

The White Hart, with Frank presiding as the life and soul of the party, was always packed. I became something of a regular and also provided stabling at Edbrookes for his wife Penny's horse. Frank also owned the Taw River Inn at Sticklepath on the A30 just east of Okehampton, which was run by his brother Mike. The pub had a golf team, for which I played on many occasions, and great fun we had.

But there was another side to Frank. One Friday morning, as I was driving him to Burnham, he turned to me and said that he wanted me to do something for him, and I was more than taken aback when he explained that the something in question was to speak at his funeral, assuring me in the process that there was absolutely nothing wrong with him but that there would come a time. Which turned out to be 25 years later when, out of the blue, he committed suicide. No-one really knew why, but Penny hadn't forgotten his request and I duly, and with some difficulty, gave the eulogy to a packed crematorium. Dear old Frank. He was much missed.

But back to Burnham. The arrival of the motorway made the golf club much more accessible but also started a chain of events which was to have profound consequences for Burnham and Berrow GC. The work coincided with the club's decision to construct a new nine-hole course between the main course and the sea, and someone had the bright idea of using waste from the motorway construction to help create the new fairways. It was supposed to be topsoil but proved to contain all manner of rubbish, and most of it had to be removed at great expense.

The Burnham membership was not large in the 1970s, certainly not large enough or wealthy enough to raise a levy to cover the debt which the club was facing. So the options came down to taking out a loan to cover the losses or selling the 13th hole on the championship course for housing development. A Special General Meeting was called to decide the way forward. As someone who had built his entire, very successful, farming business on borrowed money and understood the enduring value of land, the prospect of the club taking out a loan bothered me not one bit. So at the meeting I stood up and said as much, concluding with "Gentlemen, please don't sell real estate."

But I was in the minority. "Sit down," a chorus of members cried out. "You've only been a member for five minutes." So the decision to sell the land was taken and has been regretted ever since.

My next run-in with the club's management came in 1984, when I received the papers for the AGM and looked at the balance sheet. It seemed to me straightaway that the club was technically broke. So I rang my accountant, Keith Keyte, who was also a Burnham member, and asked him to take a look. He agreed with me, so I suggested we set up a meeting with the club chairman, Bruce Parsons, to express our very real concerns. When I rang Bruce to say that Keith Keyte and I would like a meeting, his first response was to say that Keith was no friend of his. "So what's that got to do with it?" I replied. "This is about the survival of Burnham and Berrow Golf Club."

But he did agree to the meeting, at Keith's house in West Monkton. When the two were introduced the chairman said as they shook hands "I don't believe we've met", an admission, in the light of his previously proclaimed antipathy, which seemed to me to encapsulate everything that was wrong with the way the club was being run.

The meeting seemed to have got us nowhere, and there was little support for our concerns among the committee. So we decided to collect the 65 signatories we needed to call a Special General Meeting, something we achieved with remarkably little difficulty. The SGM when it came was a traumatic affair, not made any easier for me by the fact that it was held on the very same day that I cremated my father, who had died at the age of 87.

I acted as spokesman for the 65 dissenters, as we were seen. It ended with us being told that if we didn't like the way the club was being run, then we should try to run it ourselves, a challenge which I think our opponents were expecting us to duck. But they found me a lot more determined than they had imagined.

I took over as chairman of the club's committee, with Keith Keyte as Treasurer. My first task was to tell Harry Jackson, our distinctly volatile secretary, that his time was up. It was a difficult encounter which thankfully ended with a handshake. Harry's pension was agreed along with life membership of the club, a gesture which it soon appeared wasn't universally approved of by the membership. In the event, however, Harry only appeared once afterwards, so all was well in the end. We appointed his assistant, Elizabeth Sloman, as his successor, who was unsure of herself at first but turned out to be one of the best Secretaries the club has ever had.

Meanwhile Keith was getting to grips with the club's finances, which were dire. The 13th hole was sold to two members for what seems now as the pitiful sum of £80,000, but even with that the position was far from secure and we spent many hours agonising over whether we could afford to keep the new Channel Course, as it was called. There was still a good deal of suspicion in the air, particularly among the old guard, and our proceedings were closely scrutinised by the President, Mac Brown, the Vice-President, Alec Hamilton (the retired Bishop of Jarrow) and a senior member called George Williams. All of this scrutiny did tend to prolong meetings unnecessarily, but on the whole their input was helpful and supportive as well as helping to rebuild harmony within the club.

We were also in need of a head greenkeeper, a position most effectively filled by Lauchlan 'Jock' Millar, who happily lived just up the road in Berrow, so saving us the expense of providing accommodation. With Jock's arrival and the appointment of new stewards in Andrew Nimmo and his wife Jane, it was the beginning of a happy period for the club. Over the next ten years Keith sorted out the finances, agreeing wages and pensions with the staff; all of the machinery was updated and some £200,000 was invested against future rainy days. Sincere thanks are owed to Keith, whose financial management arguably saved the club from bankruptcy, to Elizabeth Sloman for her quiet and always friendly efficiency, to Gordon Copley, who shared chairmanship duties with me, and to our committee who steered Burnham through distinctly stormy waters to the happy and stable club which it became.

To have been able to help turn around the club that I loved would have been reward enough for me, so being asked to be Captain during our centenary year of 1990 was the icing on the cake. The year began with a service in St Mary's in Berrow, where Alec Hamilton preached, David Lloyd Jenkins played the organ, complete with a piece that he had composed for the occasion, while our Lady Captain, Alison Smith, and I read lessons. That was a very happy and very special occasion, as was the Centenary Dinner, at the County Hotel in Taunton, where Sir Robin Butler, the Cabinet Secretary, who had been a member of the club when he was a teacher at St Christopher's prep school and who also played rugby for Bridgwater, was our main speaker.

Another highlight was a three-way match with two other clubs which were celebrating their centenaries, Bristol & Clifton and Royal Porthcawl, whose captain, by happy coincidence, was Leo McMahon, an old school friend of mine. It was a memorable year.

Three golf captains
Bristol & Clifton, Burham & Berrow, Royal Porthcawl

Burnham and Berrow Golf Club Centenary Dinner, 1990
Elizabeth Sloman, Sir Robin Butler, Alison Smith, Alec Hamilton, Lady Butler, Wesley Wyatt,
Olive Wyatt, Mac Brown, Alma Brown, Gordon Copley, Edna Williams, Tony Hill, George Williams

That wasn't quite the end of my involvement in the governance of Burnham and Berrow GC. In the mid-1990s, I played golf at the Rolls of Monmouth, a fine club on the Welsh border, where the members had been offered £500 apiece to sell their club to an outside consortium. Much the same sort of thing was happening to other clubs at the time, so it seemed to me to be prudent to re-cast our constitution to protect Burnham against such a risk. Three prominent members, Dick Champion, Geoffrey Stocks and Keith Keyte, were given the task and the result of their labours has protected Burnham as a members' club ever since.

Mention of Geoffrey Stocks brings me to the Stocks group, which plays foursomes at Burnham every Wednesday morning, come hell or high water, followed by a good lunch! It was started by Geoffrey and another great character called Bryden Henderson, who had once played rugby in the front row for Scotland. I joined in around 1998 and have been a regular ever since, revelling, not just in the golf but in the comradeship and conversation of a group of admittedly fairly senior golfers, who have seen and achieved much, not just in golf but in their lives more generally. It is a group of which it has been an enormous pleasure and a great privilege to be part.

The Stocks group covers a broad spectrum of golfing expertise, from former winners of the President's Putter and ex-Presidents of the EGU through to honest battlers like myself. One of the best golfers to have featured was Tony Beech, whom I had met in 2005 and arranged for him to join the group. Two Stock tours were particularly memorable thanks to Tony. The first, in 2007, took in West Sussex, a fine course with a particularly frightening 6th hole, involving a 200-yard carry over water. When we reached the tee, Tony, as was his wont, took three clubs from his bag, selected one of them, teed his ball and, without further ado, hit his shot to within six feet of the hole.

The second tour was to Scotland, and this time it wasn't the golf which was memorable so much as the travel arrangements. We flew from Bristol to Inverness, Tony presenting his gun licence by way of proving his identity. Then, when it came to the return journey, he became very agitated over how he was going to accommodate on the plane all of the teddy bears that he had bought for his daughter. We obliged by bringing them all back on the back seat of the car!

Another Stocks regular is Dr Nick Kippax, a much-loved retired GP from Wedmore. We both enjoy the Open Championship and twice, when it was held at Royal Birkdale on the Lancashire coast, we travelled up together for the first day. On the first occasion, arriving early, I left my possessions with the professional, Brian Hodgkinson, who had been Richard Bradbeer's assistant pro at Burnham. But when I came back at lunchtime to collect my stuff, the barriers were up and no way were the security men going to let me through. As I was wondering what on earth to do next, I spotted a smartly dressed gentleman coming out of the clubhouse. Thinking he might be some sort of prominent member, I waved to him. He waved back and came over to see what was going on. Taking a bit of a punt, and knowing that Nick Kippax was well-connected at Royal Birkdale, I said to him: "You must be Dr Kippax's friend." I am, he replied, and the gates were opened.

In conversation as we walked towards the clubhouse, I mentioned to him that I had never been able to find the plaque commemorating the shot that Arnold Palmer had played in winning the Championship in 1961, out of a bush and onto the 16th green. "There's a photograph of it in the locker room," he replied. "Let's go and take a look." As we walked through the door, who should be coming out but Tom Watson? Never having been backward in coming forward, I said to him, "Hello, Tom, how are you?" as if I'd known him all my life.

Not in the least bit taken aback, he replied, "I'm well, thank you. And how are you?" whereupon I shook the biggest hand I have ever shaken.

On the second occasion I contacted Richard Bradbeer to say that Dr Kippax and I would be coming to the first day of the Open. Without any prompting he said immediately that he would arrange tickets for us to use the clubhouse and would meet us there. He was as good as his word. Nick Kippax and I lunched that day at a table in the big bow window overlooking the 18th green – the best seats in the house!

Richard Bradbeer was a legend in the golfing world. His father Bob, who had been the pro at Burnham and Berrow for many years, was one of eight Bradbeer brothers, born and brought up just along the road from the golf club, all of whom became professional golfers. Richard learned his trade as a caddy, then followed in his father's footsteps, first at Taunton and Pickeridge, then at Bristol and Clifton, then back to Burnham before ending his career at Royal Birkdale, where they thought so highly of him that they made him President of the club when he retired! I can think of no comparable instance, and it just shows the enormous respect in which he was held by the membership.

The Burnham connection also accounted for my only really memorable rugby occasion. This was in 1981 when Harry Jackson, the golf club secretary, who had played rugby for Ulster, arranged for a group of us to travel to Dublin for the Ireland/England international and to attend the Irish Wolfhounds dinner on the evening before. The Wolfhounds were basically the Irish second team, and they knew how to drink. The dinner was billed as 7.30 for 8. We sat down at 11, and the speeches, from Tony O'Reilly and Cliff Morgan, were still going at one in the morning! I was presented with a Wolfhounds tie and made an associate member. The following afternoon, after the match, we were taken to the Shelburne Hotel, where literally hundreds of pints of Guinness were waiting for all-comers. What a weekend that was!

My only other sporting foray of any note was into horse racing. It was one of the keenest Stocks, John Tucker, who farmed just along the road from the golf club, who in the early 1990s persuaded a few of us to become racehorse owners. His friend Jim Old, who trained very successfully at Barbury Castle, had a horse called Certain Style and was looking for an owner for it. John had the horse in his paddock on his farm at Brent Knoll and invited a group of us with our wives to come and take a look and discuss ownership.

With some misgivings, but carried along by John's enthusiasm, I agreed and took out a share. The next stage was an early morning visit to Jim Old's yard to see Certain Style being put through his paces. First impressions were favourable, as our horse outpaced the rest on his first circuit. But then Jim instructed the jockey to take him round again. Certain Style just stood there, shook his head and refused to move. I very much feared at that moment that we had bought a pup.

And so it proved. Certain Style had ability, but a mind of his own. He did come third in a race at Wincanton, but after that, wherever we tried him, Cheltenham included, he refused to start. So our foray into racing was a disappointment. When it comes to making money, sheep are a much better bet than horses!

Jim Old with Certain Style – a horse with a mind of its own

11

From bulldozers to stewardship

One of the first things I did when I took over the farm from father was to start thinking about how to how to turn our 100 or so acres, with an average field size of four acres, into something that was manageable and viable. My father loved his hedges. The locals used to say that you could always tell where Dick Wyatt was on his farm by the plumes of smoke sent skywards from the bonfires that he lit to burn the cuttings left behind from laying or trimming his hedges. As a young man with ambition this sort of approach didn't fit with me at all. Besides, all the hundreds of hours I'd spent going around the farm, trimming the hedges with a staff hook, certainly concentrated the mind when it came to the pros and cons of small fields!

One of the first areas I looked at was what we called 'the moor', about two acres of boggy land on the northern bank of the Hillfarrance Brook. It was as good as useless. If a horse tried to walk through it, it would sink to its belly in mud and water. When I started spuddling about down there, I found the remains of all sorts of drainage pipes, all broken and useless. So I put together a plan to drain the land, backed by a generous Ministry of Agriculture grant, good drainage being regarded as one of the key requirements for productive farming. This obviously involved putting new land drains in, but we also had to lower and straighten the brook to create the necessary gradient.

The plans could have been even more ambitious, because Joe Leigh-Firbank, who owned the land on the southern side of the brook, which he called Croford Moor, was equally concerned about his drainage or lack of it. By a happy coincidence Somerset County Council were just at that time planning to widen the bridge which carried an increasingly busy A361 (as was) across the brook. They offered to carry out the work in a way which would assist the drainage of all the surrounding land, if the riparian owners on both sides of the bridge (a) agreed to the scheme and (b) were prepared to contribute modestly to the extra cost. There were four of us owners: Joe Firbank, Clifford Tudball from West Brook, Bill Rawle and me. We set up a meeting to discuss the scheme and, hopefully, strike a deal. Joe, Clifford and myself arrived in good time and waited for Bill to appear. Eventually he arrived, bringing with him his grand-daughter. "I've got a statement to make," he announced. "If I've got any money, I'm not going to let you buggers have it. Thic little maid is going to get it." And with that, he turned on his heel and left. He was as good as his word. His 'little maid' did indeed inherit his money – millions of it. But it put the mockers on any chance of draining the land upstream of the bridge.

That done, I turned my attention to the rest of the farm. The four little orchards were the first to go. Grubbed up and burnt. The pittance we got from Hancocks for the apples was never enough to make the cost and labour of pruning and harvesting worthwhile, and, being old, standard orchards, they tended only to crop properly every other year. The man who did the work was Ron Deer from Chipstable, who drove a Caterpillar D6 bulldozer for the contractors Manthorpes. Once he'd finished with the orchards, he moved onto the hedges, taking out just about every internal field boundary, hedgerow trees and all. It must have nearly broken father's heart to see it, but I had no qualms. I needed to create a manageable unit and, besides, wasn't it clear government policy, under-scored by the hedge removal grants, to increase field size and so boost productivity from the land? I was simply doing my duty by the nation – and saving myself a lot of unproductive drudgery in the process.

The first time that it dawned on me that I could perhaps have gone a little too far in my crusade to turn the farm into a prairie was in 1959, when a spark from the firebox of a steam locomotive started a crop fire. Some of the wheat had been harvested, the straw stacked in stooks, and some of it was standing uncut. It made no difference. The whole lot went up in smoke. And because there were no hedges, there was nothing to stop the flames engulfing the whole of Croford Hill. Quite apart from raising questions over the wisdom of total hedge removal, that was also my first experience of loss adjusters for insurance companies. My insurers, NFU Mutual, used experienced local farmers to do this job. My cousin, Fred Elliott, did the job very fairly for many years. But the farmer I got, who came from Stogumber way, might just as well have been a salaried member of staff. He seemed more interested in what I'd saved than what I'd lost. I wouldn't have to harvest the uncut corn; I wouldn't need to haul the grain and straw; I wouldn't need to thresh the sheaves; and so on. By the time he'd finished it seemed to me that it wouldn't have been worth growing all that corn in the first place!

If that gave me pause for thought, then so did what tended to happen whenever we had a spell of heavy rain. The soil on the slope of Croford Hill is a medium sandy loam on a clay base, very productive if properly managed but inclined to erosion in wet weather. Not far away at Burchers Farm, Milverton, which is much steeper than Hillacre, I remember Grandfather Reed with his three-wheeled truck, into which he would shovel soil at the bottom of his steeper fields, leaving his horses to haul it to the top, for him to tip the truck over, the soil being safely restored to the top of the field. It didn't quite come to that with us, but a period of heavy rain in winter would leave us with deep gullies, where the soil had been washed off our giant prairie and into the Hillfarrance Brook, next stop the river Tone and the Somerset Levels.

We took to using a turnover plough to push the soil uphill, but it wasn't until the advent of Fitzhead Farms and the influence of Chris Shapland that my self-inflicted problem was satisfactorily solved. Chris was a natural conservationist, who liked nothing better than to integrate nature into the way he farmed. He saw the solution almost immediately: put some of the hedges back in but planted along the contours of the hill, to hold the soil, rather than up and down the slope. So this was what we did, from the early 1970s onwards. There weren't any grants for this sort of thing at that time, but the work more than paid for itself by vastly reducing the loss of soil and, sometimes, crop as well.

The railway was another factor in the equation. When it was built, back in the 1870s, a clause had been included in the Act to the effect that if and when the land on which it was built was no longer needed for the railway, it would revert to whoever the owner was at the time of closure, at no cost and including the trackbed and fencing. So when the end of the Devon and Somerset came in 1966, I was quick to take possession and Ron Deer and his D6 were once again in business to clear the ground. Before long, only the slight ridge along the side of the hill remained to show where the line once ran.

When Chris Shapland looked at the lie of the land he saw immediately the possibilities for tree planting, and we must have planted hundreds of trees in the 1970s, preserving the line of the track in the process. People say to me these days that it was a mistake to allow trackbeds to be obliterated when the Beeching axe fell and that the permanent way should have been protected against the day when cross-country railways might be needed again, whether for recreation or as an alternative to cars and buses. But with the best will in the world, it is very hard to see how a 43-mile railway, connecting two towns of modest size, which had hardly ever made a profit in its history, could ever be an economic proposition again. You will have gathered by now that whether it's hedges, orchards or railway lines, I don't have much room for sentiment!

The wheel of farming change turned full circle in 2017, when I signed a Countryside Stewardship agreement covering most of Hillacre Farm. The thinking behind it was to restore some of the habitat that has been lost over the years and create new areas for wildlife, without seriously reducing the productivity of the farm. So the land alongside the Hillfarrance Brook that I had so painstakingly drained – partly at the taxpayer's expense – in the 1950s has been put down to a mixture of legume and herb-rich sward, with another long narrow field running along the hillside a little way further up being returned to permanent pasture with very little in the way of inputs like fertiliser. In time we are hoping that this will allow wild flowers to regenerate, as well as providing an ideal habitat for ground-nesting birds. Just to the east we have built a new hedgebank to separate an area of infield grass strips from the biggest arable field on that side of the farm, so absorbing any run-off and filtering it before it reaches the brook. The vegetation on the top of the new earth bank will be cut and laid in the traditional fashion, as will another new hedge to the north of the farm buildings.

And as well as all that, we have sown a small area of the farm with a 'nectar flower mix', which the bees simply love.

For all of that, we are being modestly rewarded (especially when you take into account all the paperwork involved), but I am more than happy with the way it is working out. The farm is as productive as probably it has ever been, and we are putting something back into what they like to call 'biodiversity'. I'm sure that Chris Shapland is looking down approvingly from on high, as it was really his influence which started us on the road of finding a happy medium between productive farming, which was my speciality, and sympathetic countryside management, which was Chris's. It was in many ways the perfect partnership, as was recognised in 1988 when Fitzhead Farms became one of the first winners of the Bronze Otter award, given by the Somerset Farming and Wildlife Advisory Group (FWAG), for farming and conservation.

At Chris' funeral the address included a quotation from Henry van Dyke:

> He that planteth a tree is a servant of God. He provideth
> a kindness for many generations, and faces that he hath
> not seen shall bless him.

It could not have been more appropriate.

The hedgerows removed and restored

12

Out to grass

In 1997 Olive retired from her position as PA to the Chief Executive of Taunton Deane Borough Council and came to work with me and Reg Westcott on the farm. By this stage the main business was producing Aberdeen Angus finished cattle for Waitrose, and Olive took charge of the calf rearing, thoroughly enjoying the idiosyncrasies and characters of her charges.

Farmers Wesley & Olive Wyatt from **Somerset** are two of our specially selected farmers who produce **Aberdeen Angus Beef** for us

Wesley & Olive Wyatt, Somerset

The Angus calves were supplied by Farm Mark, and I also bought some Angus x British Friesian calves from Mary Mead at Blagdon, so they were all top quality and the business paid well. Having reared the calves since they were on the bucket at only a few weeks old, their welfare was very much a concern to both of us. Transport was arranged by Farm Mark, and the finished bullocks were loaded at night in pens of five and always travelled well in one of Gordon Gilder's lorries. As for the abattoir, at Pontefract, it could not have been more reassuring. It was set up in such a way that the pens for cattle arriving at the plant were completely out of smell and sight from the stunning area, so that animals within minutes of slaughter were lying quietly, chewing the cud. The whole set up was based on the highest welfare standards and reflected very well on Waitrose as a company.

All this came to an end in 2005 when Reg Westcott decided to retire and I had to go into hospital for knee surgery. So we ceased trading and the farm is now run (very well) by Rodney Thorne and family, who produce beef cattle and lambs for the family's butchery business in Wiveliscombe. They also farm Robert's land and the family trust land, all to a very high standard.

Gardening, reading and travelling are my main retirement pleasures. It is often said that farmers make poor gardeners, but that certainly hasn't been the case with our family. My own father was a keen and expert vegetable grower who kept us supplied the year round. Grandfather Reed, with his attention to detail, was a superb gardener, and my mother inherited much of his skill and added to it her own very special talent, which was in floral art. I well remember, aged about ten, driving the carthorse Blossom to the Recreation Ground on Wiveliscombe Flower Show day in a cart filled with great bathfuls of flowers, for which my mother won any number of floral art awards.

Laying out our new garden at Tommy Brewers was very much a joint effort, for Olive enjoys her gardening just as much as I do. The soil is grade one, and just about anything will grow quickly and happily in it. When we first started planting small plants, shrubs and trees, we had a weed-free garden, but then we bought some plants which turned out to be sharing their soil with bits of bindweed root, and we've been wrestling with the wretched stuff ever since. But even with that, I am very pleased with how our efforts have turned out, and the garden gives both of us enormous pleasure.

As for reading, I suppose my first love is Dickens. I was introduced to him by the late Richard Eyre, a lovely man who had been Dean of Exeter Cathedral, one Wednesday morning when we were playing golf together. "Read 'Bleak House'," he advised. So I did and have never looked back, having now read all 16 of Dickens' novels, some more than once. Thomas Hardy is another favourite and I greatly enjoyed Anthony Gibson's 'With Magic in my Eyes', which links Hardy and many other West Country writers to the landscapes that inspired them. But perhaps the book which has made the greatest impression on me was 'No Ordinary Time – The Story of Franklin and Eleanor

Roosevelt' by Doris Kearns Goodwin. It was recommended to Olive as a Christmas present for me when we were sailing back from the USA after visiting Hyde Park, the Roosevelts' home on the Hudson River. It is a must-read.

And then there is John Betjeman, whose work I got to know through Paul Wickham, a neighbour and Old Tauntonian, when he was suffering from motor neurone disease. I would visit him most weeks and on one occasion asked him what he would like me to do when he could no longer speak. "Read Betjeman to me," he said. So I did, and many was the smile his poems produced, on both of our faces. There is much to smile about in Betjeman.

Olive and I both love travelling, my 'travel gene' having been inherited from my mother. Our early trips were to South Africa, where cousin Mary King lived in Cape Town. For the first one we travelled by the Blue Train, which was fabulously well organised, and were met at the station by Mary. "We have to do two things," she announced as we stepped off the train. "One is to go up the mountain now, while there are no clouds; and the other is to see where your parents disembarked from the Northern Star when they visited."

On our third trip to Cape Town we had arranged to take Mary to Hermanus, on the coast to the south-east of Cape Town, for a few days' break. But when we got to our hotel, there was a note to say that Mary was in hospital after being mugged and having her handbag stolen. She was in her 70s, and she never really recovered from the attack.

Going on cruises has been a particular pleasure, especially on the 'Island Sky'. Nine times we've sailed on her, to all sorts of destinations, making many lasting friendships in the process. Our most recent trip on her was from Poole in Dorset, in the company of Bryan and Jean Patterson, celebrating their Diamond Wedding Anniversary during the voyage.

In 2002 we flew to New Zealand, stopping off at Los Angeles and the idyllic Cook Islands on the way. We got to see a lot of both North and South Islands in what is a wonderful country. At one point on the journey I was required to demonstrate how to milk a cow by hand. We might have stayed longer, to watch the finals of the national seven-a-

Our garden

side rugby tournament in Wellington and were even offered tickets by the Captain of the All Blacks, but the travel arrangements didn't quite work out. As it was, I was fascinated by some of the no-frills farming we saw on the South Island, and we got to see an albatross as well.

Our cruise to the east coast of the USA in 2015 was particularly memorable for our trip up the Hudson River to Hyde Park, which had been the home and museum of Eleanor and Franklin Roosevelt. New York at night was something I'll never forget. On that occasion we decided to travel back on the Queen Mary, to avoid jet lag. It turned out to be a good decision. I walked two miles around the ship every day without seeing a bird, a fish or even another ship until we passed the Isles of Scilly.

Having enjoyed our visit to Antarctica in 2004, where we had to give way to penguins and have the guano washed off our boots every time we rejoined the ship, we decided we would go to the other end of the earth in 2017 and see what the Arctic had to offer. What a trip this was! We boarded our ship, the Discovery, at Longyearbyen in Spitzbergen and cruised around the archipelago for 12 unforgettable days. Taking advantage of 24 hours of daylight, we saw polar bears, arctic foxes, walrus, five species of whale and countless birds. Puffins were nesting on the cliff edges, rather than in burrows. The crew and tour guides must have been delighted, because the previous cruise had been fog-bound. On a visit to the bridge of the ship, I was introduced to the First Officer, who said that he remembered me from a cruise on the Island Sky some year previously.

Fellow Stocks golfers have enlivened a good many trips, including the one to Ireland in 2017, where we were joined by Paul Forrest and his wife Jo for dinner in Dublin to celebrate Paul's 70th birthday. Then there was the trip down the Canal du Midi. It was for three couples, so I decided that the first two Stocks golfers I bumped into at Burnham on the following Wednesday would get first refusal. They turned out to be Bryan Patterson and Nick Kippax, and they both accepted on the spot. We had a splendid time, Nick Kippax and I taking bicycles to visit the vineyards that we passed, although the French system of braking by reverse pedalling took some getting used to as did riding on the right.

April 16 2022 was my 90th birthday, which we celebrated with two splendid lunches, superbly arranged by Olive, at the Castle Hotel in Taunton. The first, on the day itself, was for close friends and family, including my three cousins from the Netherlands. On the following day we visited Stogumber church, where their grandparents, Nell and Henry, were married in 1914.

To the second, on April 19th we invited all of the members of the Stocks group and their wives, including Anne Eyre and Jane Henderson. It was a truly memorable occasion. Anthony Gibson proposed my health and a good time was had by all. Jill and Richard Evans had kindly arranged for a photographer to be on hand to record the occasion, and in the album with which I was subsequently presented every single photograph shows happiness, laughter and smiles – something which seemed to reflect perfectly all the laughter, happiness and smiles which the Stocks group has given us over the years, both on the golf course and off it.

90th birthday celebrations with Olive and Anthony Gibson

13

Health and happiness

Writing this at the age of 90, I can but thank God and my genes for what has been, for the most part, a healthy as well as a long life. But I've had my issues along the way, starting way back in the 1950s when I was plagued with nasal polyps. I was under the care of Peter Huggill, an ear, nose and throat specialist, who eventually sorted the problem but only after at least four visits. On one occasion, when I was particularly desperate, I asked if I could see him the next day as a private patient. He told me he didn't do private work, so I offered to pay him in potatoes if he would break the habit of a lifetime. This obviously tickled him and he agreed. So I arrived the next day with two bags of potatoes. "I only want one," he said. But he did, as I say, finally sort the problem out by operating to remove the polyps under a general anaesthetic. When I came round, I seemed to have at least a yard of bandage in each of my nostrils. This was unceremoniously and very painfully removed by a New Zealand nurse who told me not to be such a baby when I cried out in pain.

Then there were my eyes. I hadn't realised quite how bad they were until 1992, when I was visited by Michael Willacy, Secretary of the Old Tauntonians, who had a report for me to read. He was horrified when I went to get my magnifying glass so I could make out the words on the page and arranged an appointment for me to see his brother-in-law, an eye specialist, in Manchester. He, in turn, referred me to an eye surgeon, Alan Ridgeway, telling me that he would provide me with better sight than I'd been born with. This turned out to be quite true, although, coward that I am, I insisted on having the treatment done under general anaesthetic, something I was made to feel rather ashamed of when I turned up at the surgery the morning after the operation to encounter five ladies, all of whom had had their cataracts done under local anaesthetic and apparently hadn't felt a thing! Six months later I had the second eye done, this time under local anaesthetic, and from not being able to pick out a golf ball in flight before the operations, now I can see a ball 400 yards away.

Knee surgery in 2005 was life-changing. I had been struggling with my knees for years, getting more and more lame and in pain a lot of the time. This came to a head on a golfing trip to Northern Ireland in the spring of 2005 when I found myself barely able to walk. So when I got back, I rang my surgeon, Mr Kelly, and told him that the time had come for the knee transplants we had been discussing. The plan was to have the first knee done on 12 August and the second six days later. The first operation went well and, when the time came for the second, he and his anaesthetist stood at the end of my bed and asked me if I was in any pain. I said no. Whether that was the trigger or something else, he decided to put me on a machine which monitored my blood movements, and this revealed a blood clot, which might have killed me if it had passed unnoticed. It meant that the operation had to be postponed until November, but it turned out to be a complete success and gave me a new lease of life.

Jayne and her husband Shaun

Me and Robert
Tom, Hugh and James

Jayne and Olive

14

Concluding thoughts

I am grateful to Anthony Gibson for persuading me to write about my life. It has brought back many memories and provoked much thought about the familial genes which have made me the person I am.

There is no doubt that the major influence in my life has been my mother. We often didn't see eye to eye but she was a decision-maker who set and expected the highest moral standards from those around her. The decision-making I like to think I have inherited and, if I haven't matched her religious convictions, I have at least tried to emulate my mother in her truthfulness, consideration for others and her commitment to service before self. She was respected by everyone in our extended family, even her brother George, who was a bit of a black sheep, perhaps over-fond of a pint of Bass, who liked nothing better than to breathe his alcoholic fumes over my mother whenever he kissed her.

My mother's faith was impregnable and gave her great strength. When her health began to fail her, she told me in a matter of fact way that she would have to go into hospital but not, please, before her birthday on March 31. She went into Musgrove Park in early April and by the middle of the month she was dead. She must have known that she was dying, but then death held no fear for her. She knew that she was going to a better place.

My other big influence has been Donald Crichton-Miller, my headmaster at Taunton School and a great friend and mentor in later life. He reflected and reinforced many of my mother's standards, as well as instilling in me the essentials of politeness, dress code, courtesy and consideration for others. If I am rarely seen in company in anything other than jacket and tie; if I make a point of holding doors open for others; if I am straightforward and honest in my dealings; and if I greet strangers and friends alike with a firm, friendly but respectful handshake, then Crikey set the example.

As I write, the sound of gunfire is echoing across the fields, aimed at game birds which have been reared for the purpose. Whilst I most certainly regard myself as a countryman, I do have serious misgivings about some of the activities which are traditionally associated with country life. Shooting for the sake of it as opposed to shooting for the pot is one, hunting is another.

Retirement has given me plenty of time to reflect, on my own life and on the world in which we live. I have to admit that my Christian faith, once so strong, has been badly shaken by some of the things that have happened and by some of the people responsible for them, in my lifetime. In Chapel we sing: "This, this is the God we adore." But where is he, and can my God be the same God they worship in the Russian Orthodox Church, which has given its blessing to the outrages being committed by the tyrant Putin in Ukraine?

"Man's inhumanity to man makes countless thousands mourn," wrote Robert Burns. They are words which come to mind far too often when I look back at some of the terrible things that have happened over the past 80 years, most of them stemming from the egos of dictators; the likes of Stalin, Hitler, Hirohito, Pol Pot, Mugabe and now Putin. Some of the things I saw in the prisoner-of-war museum in Japan when Olive and I visited the Bridge on the River Kwai defied description. How can a caring God allow these things to happen, these men – and they are all men – to exist and prosper?

I remember driving Richard Eyre, the Dean of Exeter Cathedral and the best sort of Christian, past Peterborough Cathedral and asking him whether it had been built by faith or by fear. His answer: "Wesley, I am resting my eyes."

But there is another side to the coin, which was brought home to me at a party given to mark the retirement of Lee Glaser as Headmaster of Taunton School. Among several inspirational remarks he related the story of a Ukrainian former pupil who had come back to visit the school and had been warmly greeted and embraced by a Russian former school-friend. It did my old heart good to hear it and maybe restored just a smidgeon of my faith in human nature.

Looking back on my farming career, I see a lifetime of progress. Farming is far more efficient and less labour-intensive (horticulture excepted) than it was when I started. Before we bought our first tractor, a Standard Fordson, in 1941, ploughing was done by one man, two horses and a single turnover plough. One acre a day was good going, and 10 per cent of the farm was down to hay and oats to feed the horses. By 1970 Reggie Westcott was ploughing ten acres a day for me at Brewers or Hillacre, and these days, 30 acres is by no means unusual (the 24 hour record is actually 226 acres!).

The story hasn't just been one of bigger and better machines. Advances in soil management have seen the plough being gradually superseded by minimal cultivation regimes, without any damage to yields, which have continued to increase thanks to better varieties, sprays and fertilisers. Although thinking of fertilisers, what has happened since Putin's invasion of Ukraine ought to provide food for serious thought. Is it sensible to be as reliant as we obviously are on importing fertilisers from less than friendly countries, when we could be making better use of our own animal manures? – always provided the anti-beef and dairy brigade don't succeed in drastically reducing the numbers of sheep, cattle, pigs and poultry which provide it!

In livestock farming I suppose the biggest step forward has been in breeding, thanks to the use of artificial insemination and embryo transfer. Sheep farming has been revolutionised by the use of Texel and Beltex rams, even if they do produce lambs which are far too lean for fat-lovers like me!

Although I would always vote against government interference in agriculture, it would be foolish to pretend that government subsidies and grants have not profoundly influenced the way I have farmed, be that hedge removal in the 50s, co-operation in the 70s and 80s or conservation in the 2000s. From the post-war calf subsidy through to the Single Farm Payment, I must have been paid hundreds of thousands of pounds in taxpayers' money – most of it, I would contend, having been put to good use in food production and countryside management. But my next government payment will be my last, because I am taking advantage of a scheme which will pay me to retire, once and for all. It is called, unromantically, the 'Lump Sum Exit Scheme', and if all goes to plan it will pay me 2.35 times the amount of Single Payment I received on average over the three years 2019-21. It won't exactly be a fortune, but it will be very welcome and it means that I can give a tenancy on the land to Rodney Thorne and his family, knowing that it will be well farmed. So I will leave farming as I entered it, carried on the wings of a government grant!

Many years ago, in an article for the *Somerset Farmer*, I concluded with the following:

> Farming will continue to be a way of life for optimists.
> We shall reach new peaks which may not be of yield, but
> if they are of quality they will be no less satisfying, and
> the weather will remain the major talking point.

Thirty-four years on, I see no reason to alter that judgement. Despite the unpredictability of some of my endeavours, I remain an optimist!